Broadcast Voice Handbook

How to Polish Your On-Air Delivery

Ann S. Utterback, Ph.D.

Medical Consultant
Barbara J. Scherokman, M.D.
Neurologist
Washington, D.C.

Broadcasting Consultant
Susan L. Stolov, President
Washington Independent Productions
Washington, D.C.

94 93 92 91 90   5 4 3 2 1

Library of Congress Catalog Card Number
90-81335

International Standard Book Number
0-929387-16-3

Bonus Books, Inc.
160 East Illinois Street
Chicago, Illinois 60611

Printed in the United States of America

Voice is probably the #1 criterion used in hiring. When News Directors punch the eject button 15 seconds into an applicant's tape, they do it because that applicant sounds like an amateur, not a professional. . . . If you're going to make your living with your voice, you should learn to use your voice effectively. It is as basic as learning how to type, and for a broadcaster it is just as important.

David Cupp
News Director, WVIR–TV
Charlottesville, Virginia

Reporters and anchors should take a much more active approach to improving their voices. It is probably the most *ignored of all broadcasting tools. It shouldn't be.*

Penny Parrish
News Director, KMSP–TV
Minneapolis, Minnesota

Courtesy of KSL–TV, Salt Lake City, UT

Courtesy of KGO Radio, San Francisco, CA

The effect of a broadcaster's voice is immediate and overpowering. No amount of excellent writing or good on-air presence can compensate for a poor voice.

Susan L. Stolov
President
Washington Independent Productions
Washington, D.C.

There is nothing magic about a good broadcast voice. Good vocal delivery is often as much the result of hard work and following the right advice as it is God-given talent.

Jack Keefe
News Director, WICD–TV
Champaign, Illinois

Contents

Quick Reference to Common Broadcast Voice Problems

Acknowledgments

A project like this is always based on the support of many people. My thanks date back twenty years to my colleagues at Memphis State University. I thank Mike Osborn for shoving a voice and diction book in my hand and telling me I was going to begin teaching voice and diction, and Jack Sloan for providing continued opportunity to teach at Memphis State. David Yellin taught me to respect the television medium and the people who work in it. Working with Yellin's friends such as Fred Freed and Paul Bogart was invaluable to my development. I am grateful to Betty May Collins Parker and Lea Queener for sharing their extensive knowledge and inspiring me with their continuing interest in the field of voice improvement.

I was fortunate to have the opportunity to attend Isaac Brackett's classes during my doctoral work at Southern Illinois University. As an outstanding speech pathologist, Dr. Brackett's help was immeasurable. The medical assistance I received from Barbara Scherokman, M.D., and Joshua Oppenheim, M.D., was essential to the integrity of this book. I appreciate their guidance and input.

News directors across the country have contributed to this project. You will see many of their names throughout the book and in Appendix B. I would especially like to thank Jim Rutledge, former Assistant Bureau Chief of the CNN Washington Bureau, who first suggested I concentrate my professional interests in broadcast voice. Mike Freedman, Managing Editor,

WWJ Radio/CBS, Inc., Detroit, Michigan, has been supportive of my work for a number of years, and I am honored to include his Foreword in this book. Brian Olson, News Director, KGWN–TV, Cheyenne, Wyoming, and Dave Cupp, News Director, WVIR–TV, Charlottesville, Virginia, have offered continuing support. J. Spencer Kinard, News Director, KSL–TV, Salt Lake City, Utah, was kind enough to provide a number of photographs for the book. I would also like to thank Sue Stolov, President, Washington Independent Productions, for her careful reading of the manuscript and for giving me confidence in my work from the very beginning.

I am grateful to the people at Bonus Books, who believed in this project and followed it from inspiration to publication.

I am indebted to the Radio-Television News Directors Association for their support of my work. Dave Bartlett, President, and Pat Seaman, Director of Meetings and Special Events, and all the Washington staff have made working with RTNDA a pleasure.

Thanks also to Toni Krochmal and Tracey Stith, two treasured friends, without whom this book could not have been completed. They were there with help and support when I needed them just as they have been many times in the past. And to B. J. and Jim, the only two people who really understand what it took to write this book, I give my thanks for enduring.

I dedicate this book to Jim whose constant love and encouragement have been the foundation for all the accomplishments in my life. He has shown me, "It can be."

Ann S. Utterback, Ph.D.
September, 1990

Foreword

The voice is to the broadcaster as the hands are to the pianist. Just as a musical score is enhanced by the expertise and enthusiasm of the artist, the written word is transformed into meaningful information for the ear by the eloquence and style of the broadcaster.

An effective broadcast voice requires training, practice, and care. The best in the profession understand their role as communicators and the importance of the voice in the process. While they do not all sound alike, they share important common traits. They are authoritative and articulate. They give each word meaning. They add dimension and perspective to stories. They know the difference between just reading copy and conveying information in a manner that draws the listener or viewer to the broadcast. It is an art. As such, the voice becomes the brush that paints pictures for the mind's eye.

Listen to the broadcasts of Edward R. Murrow from London or Walter Cronkite following the death of President Kennedy. These are classic examples of delivering an important message with professionalism. These riveting broadcasts stir emotion, yet maintain a sense of calm through calamity.

Aspiring broadcasters are advised to articulate, enunciate, breathe from the diaphragm, sound authoritative, stay calm under fire, and, all the while, be conversational! This must seem an impossible combination at first. Yet, through training, practice, and care, the voice becomes polished and the procedures routine. Notice it is usually the novice who sounds quite different on the air than off. Professionals sound the same in normal conversation as they do when the microphone is on.

Over the course of my twenty years in electronic journalism, it has been encouraging to see a renewed enthusiasm for training and care of the voice among broadcasters. A recent seminar on the subject at a Radio-Television News Directors Association International Conference drew a standing-room-only audience. That session proved to be among the most highly rated at RTNDA functions in recent years. It was moderated by Ann Utterback.

I was pleased to have recommended Ann to the RTNDA for that session, after seeing the results of her work with broadcasters in Washington, D.C. As then-managing editor for the broadcast division of United Press International, I was led to Ann in seeking a voice consultant for some of the staff members of our radio network. The improvement among those who studied with Ann was remarkable. They not only sounded better on the air, they felt better about themselves. They learned that all voices are special and distinctive and often, minor modification and practice can transform an adequate voice into an excellent one.

I am honored to have been asked to write the foreword to this excellent handbook. With it, Ann Utterback is helping to rekindle a vital light in our industry; the delivery of the message and the importance of "The Broadcast Voice."

Michael Freedman
Managing Editor, WWJ Radio/ CBS, Inc.
Detroit, Michigan
National Director-at-Large
Radio-Television News Directors Association

You only have one opportunity to get your message across to the public—if they don't understand (or get bored listening to a lackluster delivery) there are other channels to watch.

Bob Campbell
News Director, WTHR–TV
Indianapolis, Indiana

We must never forget that it is our voice only *that gives the listener an* image. . . . *We must gain the listeners' respect and trigger their imagination!*

Ray Marks
News Director, WGR AM & FM
Buffalo, New York

If you do not develop the best voice possible you are trying to do the job without the proper tools. It's like trying to do surgery with a penknife.

Don Scott
News Director, KOSA–TV
Odessa, Texas

Introduction

Assemble any group of broadcasters, and you will hear comments like these.

> "There's an anchor slot open at my station, but my news director hasn't moved me into it."

> "My resume tape keeps being returned. News directors say I show good writing skills and look great, but . . .."

> "I may lose my job as education reporter. All my news director says is I'm too stiff."

What the news directors have left unsaid in each case is that the broadcaster's voice is the problem. The broadcaster may have a thin voice that is inappropriate for an anchor position, too little vocal variety, or an overly precise delivery. All of these and many other vocal problems can be corrected with proper training and practice.

When I first began working almost exclusively with broadcasters five years ago, I had spent fifteen years teaching college students, corporate executives, and government officials how to use their voices well. I assumed broadcasters, who make their living with their voices, were trained to use their voices more effectively than most professionals.

As I began working with broadcasting clients, I realized this was frequently not the case. I saw increasing numbers of clients who did not know how to breathe correctly or use their voices to enhance the meaning of their copy. These clients ranged from recent college graduates to broadcast veterans with fifteen years of experience who had risen to the network level. Most had a basic lack of knowledge of how to care for their voices and use them effectively.

My biggest surprise came when I was asked to do a lecture at the 1988 Radio-Television News Directors Association International Conference in Las Vegas. I was told to expect around thirty participants, and that number sounded appropriate to me for a group of professionals, the majority of whom I thought knew my subject well. When three hundred participants showed up for that lecture, I realized that knowledge about how to use your voice effectively was sorely lacking in the broadcasting community throughout the country. The top rating my lecture received reinforced this conclusion.

At the RTNDA convention, broadcasters showed an enormous interest in the anatomical approach I take to voice improvement. They seemed to want all the knowledge I could give them about how to help their newscasters have healthy voices that enhance meaning.

In the questionnaire I sent to 671 news directors in preparation for this book, comments like this one from Loren Tobia, News Director, KMTV, Omaha, Nebraska, summarized for me what most news directors seem to feel: "It's great to be a good journalist but if the voice is bad the audience won't want to listen." Reading over the 124 news directors' comments in Appendix B, you will hear this sentiment repeated.

In addition to the need for voice work for professionals who are on the air, I have learned that there is much frustration among news directors about the lack of voice training that broadcast journalism students get while in college. Many of my clients had voiced this same frustration. I remember one young woman telling me her father was not pleased that he had to pay a consultant to work with her during her last semester of college when he was already paying tuition. Unfortunately, her university did not offer any assistance with voice improvement.

Timothy P. Kenny, News Director, WPDE–TV, Florence, South Carolina, works with entry-level reporters, and he has noticed the same thing:

> I've noted a tremendous weakness with delivery. Recently, I had a reporter-candidate with a Master's degree from a major journalism school. She was willing to come to work for entry-level money and certainly had the credentials, but her delivery just wasn't good enough for me.

Bob Shilling, News Director, WBAL Radio, Baltimore, Maryland, states this feeling more bluntly: "The proper use of the voice is paramount and is probably one of the most overlooked areas in college training."

This book is an attempt to provide the information that is needed in the newsroom and the classroom to help broadcasters develop and maintain healthy voices that enhance meaning. You will not find a quick technique in this book that will give you an instant broadcast voice. Breaking old habits and developing new ones takes time. In order to have a better broadcast voice, you must learn how your vocal mechanism works and practice the exercises that will allow new habits to be formed.

The days of training everyone to sound the same are gone. Luckily in this country we no longer have a set broadcast model. I call that old announcer's voice the "Ted Baxter" delivery from the character on "The Mary Tyler Moore Show." That voice is now being revived by the Jim Dial character on the "Murphy Brown" television show. Both of these characters mimic the staid, low-pitched delivery that was once a standard in broadcasting.

There is much more acceptance of different types of voices in broadcasting now than there was twenty years ago, but this acceptance does not mean that voice is not important. I hear this warning from more and more news directors. They feel that just because we aren't teaching all newscasters to sound like Edward R. Murrow, this does not negate the need for training. As Mike Cavender, News Director, WTVF, Nashville, Tennessee, puts it, "It isn't necessary to have a 'big' voice . . . but it is necessary to learn how to best use the voice you have."

Ray Carter, News Director, WMDT-TV, Salisbury, Maryland, explains this idea more completely:

> Less and less often we're seeing a deep, rich voice as a primary consideration for hiring in this country. That doesn't mean news directors take lightly the idea of voice quality—to the contrary. We're now trying to get the most out of what would have been considered "marginal" voices only a few years ago.

In order to get the most out of any voice, you must know the basic anatomy of speech and the fundamentals of how you can use your voice effectively. Basic knowledge about breathing, producing sound, resonating sound, and shaping sound into words is esssential for good vocal production. Broadcasters cannot begin to develop a method of stressing words, for example, without knowing how breathing relates to stressing.

In addition to the challenge of knowing the anatomy of speech in order to maintain a healthy voice, broadcasters need to develop a relaxed, conversational delivery. This is not an easy task, but it is what 84 percent of news directors indicate they desire (see Appendix A). What they want listeners to hear is a natural delivery in what is a very unnatural situation.

Establishing this natural, conversational delivery is not something that most people can accomplish without a systematic approach. Such a delivery involves breath control, pacing, and stress and intonation. Broadcasters must learn how to sound as if they are talking to someone when they are actually reading. And this situation dominates their work even in television, as Terry McElhatton, News Director, KNTV, San Jose, California, points out: "95% of TV news reporting is voice-over . . . competent and compelling storytellers are the people we look for, people who can not only write to video but can hold the audience with the power of their voice."

The old notion that broadcasters are "announcers" is gone. Comfortable "communicators" are what the public wants.

The challenge to broadcasters is to be able to relax enough in a tense situation to maintain a healthy voice and sound relaxed. In addition, listeners want them to pull out the meaning of the story with their voices. This is a difficult task.

This book attempts to provide the information needed to meet this challenge. The book is as simple and straightforward as possible. The contents are organized in a sequential manner. It begins with the production of the breath, which is the energy for speech, and moves through the production and resonating of sound waves to the articulation of the sound and finally the methods of stressing for meaning. The International Phonetic Alphabet is used as a method of presenting the sounds of our language. All phonetic symbols in the book appear in slash marks (e.g., /aɪ/).

It is recommended that you read the chapters in the order presented so that you will understand how the processes are interrelated. Even if you read the material quickly without completely retaining it, you will get an important basic understanding of vocal production.

In addition to gaining a basic understanding of vocal production, it is also necessary to develop a respect for your voice. After all, if you are a broadcaster you are making your living on two tiny muscles in your throat. Broadcasters need to recognize the importance of a healthy voice. Think of your voice as an instrument. Not many concert pianists would abuse their fingers, or ballet dancers their legs, but many broadcasters abuse their voices daily.

If you ask even a young ballerina about the hamstring or the Achilles tendon, she can usually tell you where it is and what it does. I do not find this basic knowledge of vocal anatomy with many of my clients. Most are amazed when they see photographs of the vocal folds and realize how delicate the tissue is. These same newscasters might suggest firing a camera person who did not know the basic mechanics of how television equipment works. They expect a camera person to have respect and knowledge of television equipment, while they lack the same respect and knowledge of their own vocal equipment.

Knowing the fundamentals of vocal production is only the beginning of the process of voice improvement. Just as a pianist and a dancer must practice daily to maintain their skill, broadcasters must learn that voice improvement is a lifetime pursuit. Maintaining a good broadcast voice takes hours of practice and a lifetime of respect.

Hopefully, the Warm-Ups at the end of each chapter will become part of your daily routine. These sections are marked with shaded pointers for easy reference. Each Warm-Up section is preceded by some exercises that help you become familiar with the chapter concepts. These are called "Focus on Breathing," "Focus on Phonation," etc.

Once you are familiar with the concept, you might want to put your favorite Warm-Ups on index cards, or a sheet of paper to post over your desk or in the sound booth to help you remember to practice them. Many of my clients find they like to do Warm-Ups while driving. It is especially helpful to do articulation Warm-Ups in the morning while driving to work. This is usually one time for practice that works in even the busiest schedule. You should find other times as well, because continued practice is of utmost importance in changing or maintaining vocal habits.

This book can serve as a lifetime reference companion as you continue to respect your voice by monitoring your vocal production throughout your career. It gives you the basic knowledge you need to maintain a healthy, effective voice.

One of the ironies of a good broadcast voice is that the better it is, the less it is noticed. Andy Cassells, Bureau Chief of Cox Broadcasting in Washington, D.C., feels strongly about this: "Voice in a news story should not be noticed. If it is, something is wrong!"

Bill Headline, Vice President and Bureau Chief of CNN's Washington bureau explains, "A broadcast voice should be trained, controlled, and modulated to the point that you are aware not of the voice but of the information that it is delivering."

A broadcaster's voice should be a medium that delivers information to the listener. It should never get in the way of this information. Only a healthy voice that is controlled by the broadcaster can be effective in this task. Through continued monitoring of your broadcast voice and practice to keep it healthy and effective, you can make your vocal instrument work for you.

WWJ radio reporter interviews Detroit Mayor Coleman Young.

Courtesy of WWJ Radio, Detroit, MI

Diaphragmatic breathing is a must in Broadcasting . . . too many people come out of school and have never heard of it!

John Rehrauer
News Director, KTHV–TV
Little Rock, Arkansas

The vast majority of applicants have had little or no professional voice training. As a result, they lack proper breathing techniques, and never achieve the voice potential they have. Very few know how to breathe from the diaphragm.

Joe Morgan
News Director, WHDH Radio
Boston, Massachusetts

Breathing— The Key to Good Vocal Production

"Try to relax." That is the advice I give clients every day. But the truth is, if you are a journalist working in broadcasting in the 1990s, it is difficult advice to follow. Radio and television news professionals work in a world of live reports, crises, and deadlines. The pressures and tension in television and radio broadcasting are enormous, and, for the most part, they are unavoidable. Many of you may feel the phrase "relaxed broadcaster" is an oxymoron.

A television reporter, for example, works on a schedule that demands tension and pressure. To meet a 5:00 p.m. news show deadline, a typical reporter has from 9:00 a.m. to around 4:30 p.m. to produce one or more packages. Most of the day the reporter runs all over the city interviewing people to develop a story. As the deadline approaches, the reporter must shoot a stand-up looking and sounding composed and in control. Voice-overs must be recorded in the sound booth as the deadline gets ever closer. The tension that has helped this reporter succeed in the fact-gathering part of the day now becomes a handicap.

A typical Washington television news bureau reporter might end the day viewing one of as many as three packages she did that day.

Courtesy of Washington Independent News, Washington, D.C.

This hectic schedule is accepted practice for broadcasters. Few other occupations demand this level of output. Most business executives have weeks between deadlines. Writers, actors, and other artists have months before they have to present their creative product. But broadcasters work with daily deadlines week after week.

For a broadcaster's voice to work effectively, relaxation is the key. Because your voice depends on various muscles in your body, it reflects the degree of tension you are feeling. Stress affects all your muscle tone, which affects posture, respiration, and voice control. A tense body usually means a tense voice.

Proper breathing can be very effective in relieving tension and improving the voice. Stress control workshops teach diaphragmatic breathing for relaxation. Natural childbirth depends on breathing to help alleviate pain. Concentrating on a long, slow inhalation/exhalation is often recommended by doctors to control the tension that exacerbates any type of pain.

A long inhalation/exhalation is also helpful in tense social situations such as a job interview, an especially rough airline flight, or before giving a speech.

Yoga and other Eastern philosophies have used breathing as part of meditation for centuries. The philosophy of yoga holds as a belief that if you can control the breath, or prana, you can control the mind. This idea can be adapted for broadcasters: If you can control the breath, you can control the voice.

Once you have learned proper abdominal-diaphragmatic breathing as described in the Focus on Breathing section, you can rely on this process to relax you. Your breath is your best ally as a broadcaster. It revitalizes the body while calming the emotions and bringing clarity to the mind. Proper breathing can help break the tension that builds for many broadcasters as their workdays progress.

Proper breathing not only relaxes you, it provides the basic energy for speech. Breathing for life and breathing for

Anchoring the afternoon drive shift at an all-news radio station involves the pressure of coordinating live reports, late-breaking stories, and deadlines by the minute.

Courtesy of WWJ Radio, Detroit, MI

speech, however, are not identical processes. Therefore, before you can begin to think of how to improve your broadcast voice by working on stress and intonation, rate, or pitch, you must first focus on the basic function of breathing.

Breathing Anatomy

In order to learn to use your breath properly as a broadcaster, you need to have an understanding of how we breathe. It is not necessary to learn all the muscles and nerves related to the respiratory system, but some basic anatomy will help you improve your breathing.

The Lungs

Most of us assume that we breathe with our lungs. Taking a deep breath is referred to as "filling up the lungs with air." What we may not know is that the lungs are not doing the work of inhalation or exhalation. We depend on various muscles in the chest and abdominal area to keep air circulating into our bodies.

The lungs are important for the transfer of oxygen and carbon dioxide to keep us alive, but without the muscles that control them they could not function. The lungs are like two large sponges in our chest. They are light and porous and would float in water much like a natural bath sponge. The lungs fill the area of the chest, or thoracic cavity, with the heart nestled between them.

Leading into each lung is a tube called a bronchus which, like a tree trunk, spreads roots, called bronchial tubes, into each lung (see Figure 1). These bronchial tubes branch into smaller and smaller tubes, bronchioles, and end as tiny air sacs. These air sacs have capillaries very close to the surface, and this is where the exchange of oxygen and carbon dioxide takes place. This exchange of gases is so fundamental in keeping us alive,

Figure 1
Anatomy Drawing of the Organs Involved in Speech

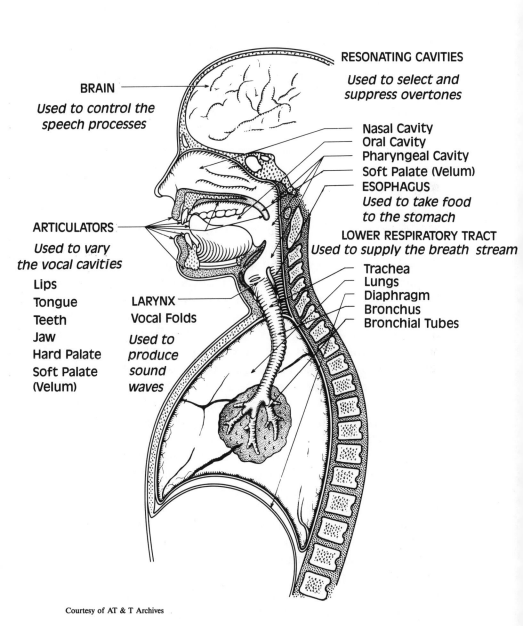

RESONATING CAVITIES

Used to select and suppress overtones

BRAIN

Used to control the speech processes

Nasal Cavity
Oral Cavity
Pharyngeal Cavity
Soft Palate (Velum)
ESOPHAGUS
Used to take food to the stomach

LOWER RESPIRATORY TRACT
Used to supply the breath stream

ARTICULATORS

Used to vary the vocal cavities

Lips
Tongue
Teeth
Jaw
Hard Palate
Soft Palate
(Velum)

LARYNX
Vocal Folds

Used to produce sound waves

Trachea
Lungs
Diaphragm
Bronchus
Bronchial Tubes

Courtesy of AT & T Archives

that it begins as a reflex action as soon as we take our first breath at birth.

Our first breath is usually accompanied by a loud cry, which indicates the close connection between breathing and speech. To produce that cry, the air exhaled from the lungs goes up the bronchial tubes into the trachea and passes through the larynx which contains the vocal folds (vocal cords) which create sound waves (see Figure 1). That air must be pushed from the lungs, however, since the lungs have no muscles themselves. This is where your understanding of the anatomy of breathing can help you as a broadcaster.

The Diaphragm

The most important muscle for speech is the diaphragm. The diaphragm muscle is a large sheet-like muscle that separates the thoracic cavity from the abdominal cavity (see Figure 2). The diaphragm bisects the body horizontally starting at the breast-bone. It continues along the bottom of the rib cage around to the spine. The diaphragm forms a complete floor for the thoracic cavity. The broad bases of our cone-shaped lungs rest on the diaphragm. This solid muscle is pierced by three important tubes: the esophagus which takes food to the stomach directly under the diaphragm, the aorta which takes blood down from the heart, and the vena cava which brings blood up from the lower part of the body to the heart (see Figure 2).

The action of the diaphragm is what allows us to breathe naturally. In its resting state, the diaphragm muscle is dome-shaped, rising up into the thoracic cavity. When we inhale with the diaphragm, this large, sheet-like muscle contracts and flattens out. As it flattens, it moves downward. The ribs flex upward at the same time. The effect of this is to increase the size of the thoracic cavity (see Figure 3). When this happens, a negative air space is created which results in a partial vacuum. Because the air pressure of our atmosphere is greater outside the body at this point, air rushes into the lungs to equalize the pressure.

Figure 2
The Thorax and Diaphragm (cut-away front view)

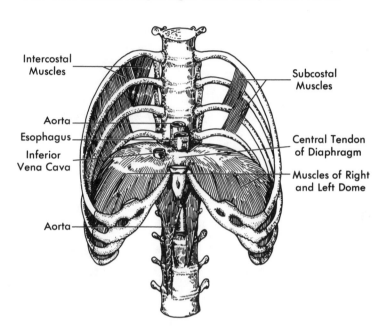

Intercostal Muscles

Subcostal Muscles

Aorta

Esophagus

Inferior Vena Cava

Central Tendon of Diaphragm

Muscles of Right and Left Dome

Aorta

From *Training the Speaking Voice*, Third Edition, by Virgil A. Anderson. Copyright © 1977 by Oxford University Press, Inc. Reprinted by permission.

As the diaphragm muscle flattens out, it also forces the abdominal area to protrude because of the pressure on the stomach, liver, spleen, and other organs beneath it. This movement of the abdominal area makes diaphragmatic breathing easy to monitor (see Focus on Breathing). With a good abdominal-diaphragmatic breath, you feel expansion in the stomach area as well as all around the back. The lower chest area may expand as much as two and one-half inches.

Once the thoracic cavity is enlarged and air has rushed into the lungs, the diaphragm and abdominal muscles work to push the air out with a controlled exhalation. Imagine a bellows filling with air. The first step is to enlarge the cavity of the bellows by separating the handles. When the bellows is filled with air, our arm muscles physically control the force of the air as it is blown out. Our abdominal muscles work much the same

Figure 3
Increase of Volume of Thorax with Inhalation

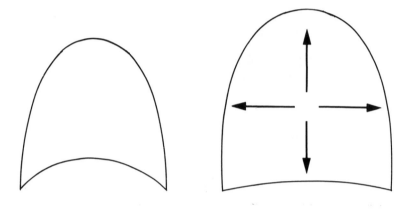

Rib cage before inhalation   Rib cage after inhalation

way by allowing the diaphragm to slowly rise back into its dome-shaped position and the rib cage to return to its original position. This movement forces air out of the lungs with control. For relaxed breathing without the demand of speech, exhalation is simply a relaxation without the control of the abdominal and diaphragm muscles. The elasticity of the rib cage and lungs contributes to the deflation of the lungs in relaxed breathing.

Respiration is a continuous process that keeps us alive. Our body cannot store oxygen. There is a constant demand for it. When our brain feels the oxygen level has dropped, a signal comes from the brain stem to replenish it. This process is so important for life, we cannot voluntarily stop it. Many children's temper tantrums have ended with the threat, "I'll hold my breath until I turn blue." The child may think this is possible, but the involuntary breathing mechanism will take over to keep the child alive.

We breathe from 15,000 to 20,000 times per day. Our lungs normally contain about three quarts of air. We generally inhale and exhale one-half quart of air in quiet respiration when we are breathing twelve to sixteen times per minute. The lungs never completely empty of air. They maintain a residual supply.

The Importance of Abdominal-Diaphragmatic Breathing

Now that you know the anatomy of breathing, you may be wondering why it is important to you as a broadcaster. If the system described above operated naturally, it would not be important. You would go through life, breathing with the diaphragm aided by the abdominal muscles, and your voice would enjoy all the benefits of this type of breathing. Unfortunately, this is not the case.

At some point in our lives we abandon this comfortable breathing for what could be called *socialized breathing*. Someone gives us the message that we should hold in our stomachs and stick out our chests. We could blame physical education teachers or army sergeants for this change, but whether we are male or female, a flat stomach and a large chest become our goals.

Knowing the basics of breathing, you can imagine the results of holding in your stomach and expanding your chest. This forces a type of breathing called upper chest, or clavicular, breathing. The muscles of the chest, or even the higher muscles in the clavicle or collarbone area and the neck muscles do the work of lifting the rib cage to expand it for breathing. Instead of using one of the largest muscles in the body, the diaphragm, which is constructed for the purpose of expanding the rib cage for breathing, we use smaller, less efficient muscles.

When I lecture to convention groups, I often ask the audience to take a deep breath. It is interesting to watch hundreds of people's shoulders heave up and down as they take what they perceive to be a deep breath. Usually only the singers or people who have played a wind instrument know that when taking a deep breath the shoulders do not move. All of the movement is in the abdominal area below the breast bone.

The fear of developing a big stomach area should not keep you from breathing properly. Ironically, abdominal-diaphragmatic breathing may result in a flatter stomach, because it calls for control of the abdominal muscles. They get a better workout when they are used for breathing than when they serve only as a girdle, constantly holding in the stomach area.

Breath Support

As a broadcaster, abdominal-diaphragmatic breathing is one of the best ways to maintain a healthy voice. If the diaphragm and abdominal muscles are doing the work during inhalation and exhalation, the tension involved in breathing is positioned far from the delicate structures in the throat which produce sound waves (laryngeal area). The movement involves the abdominal area moving out and in (see Focus on Breathing). Clavicular breathing, on the other hand, causes the shoulders to rise during inhalation, and increases muscular tension in the neck which may affect the laryngeal area. (Chapter 2 explains the importance of keeping tension away from the larynx and vocal folds.) In addition, clavicular breathing is shallow breathing, which can be exhausting.

The diaphragm and abdominal muscles give us both the ability to take in a large volume of air and to control exhalation. This is called **breath support**. The amount of time involved in a typical inhalation/exhalation at rest is quite different from the requirements for speech. Our ratio of inhalation to exhalation at rest is close to 1:1. We breathe in for about the same duration as we breathe out. For speech, this ratio must change to 1:5, 1:10, or even greater. In other words, exhalation time is greatly prolonged. We can control the air as it is exhaled if we let the diaphragm and the abdominal muscles do the work. Without control of exhalation, after a deep inhalation air would rush from our lungs as it does when we sigh. This is not conducive to good speech because we cannot say many words during the time it takes to sigh. The air rushes out too rapidly.

Think of a sculptor working on a new creation. Given a small amount of clay, the sculptor's choices are limited. Any sculpture created has to conform to the size of the clay. If the sculptor has a large chunk of clay, the choices are greater. All or part of the clay can be used, and the creation can be large or small depending on the sculptor's concept.

Your breath works in much the same way. When reading broadcast copy you need to have a good supply of air, and you need to be able to control that air. A good air supply gives you the raw material to produce good speech. Proper control of that air will help you mold speech into words that are interesting to hear, easily understood, and full of vocal energy.

Returning to the Natural

You may think at this point that learning to breathe with the diaphragm aided by the abdominal muscles will take months or years of training because it seems so unnatural. Actually, you breathe this way every night when you are sleeping. Have you ever watched a little baby on its back in a crib? The baby's stomach goes up and down, up and down, with each inhalation and exhalation. There is no socialized breathing here. You breathe the same way when you are sleeping, sick, or in a relaxed state, unaware of your breathing. Since none of these apply when you are broadcasting, there is some relearning that must take place, but it need not take long.

A few simple exercises will help you get back in touch with this normal, natural way to breathe. Begin first with the section in this chapter called Focus on Breathing to position your breathing properly. Once you have the correct feeling, proceed to the Breathing Warm-Ups. These should become part of your daily routine to help fight the desire to return to the socialized breathing style.

You should continue practice of abdominal-diaphragmatic breathing in order to increase your breath support. Like any muscle, the diaphragm contracts and relaxes.

And like any muscle it can be strengthened through proper exercising. In the same way that pumping iron builds your arm muscles, breathing exercises build your diaphragm and abdominal muscles.

Part of an opera singer's lifetime training is breathing exercises. A singer will spend time lying on the floor with weight on the abdominal area trying to push the weight up. Voice coaches might even put their foot on top of the weight to increase the pressure. All of this is intended to increase the control of the diaphragm and abdominal muscles. When you hear an opera singer hold a note for longer than seems humanly possible, you can bet that singer has worked many hours building breath support. You are listening to the results.

Vocal Benefits of Proper Breathing

What advantages does good breath support have for you as a broadcaster? You certainly do not need to sustain one sound for as long as Luciano Pavarotti or Placido Domingo. What you do need is enough air to be in control of what you are saying. You want to be in control of how long your sentences are and what you can do with your voice. Control of exhalation allows you to vary your delivery rate and duration of sounds. You will also be able to use pitch changes to enhance the meaning of your copy (see Chapter 5).

Poor breathing may result in choppy, disjointed speech. We have all heard broadcasters who have to take a breath pause at the wrong time. The meaning is often changed by an inappropriate pause. The effect is like the old example of "What's that in the road—a head?" In addition, you do not want your limited breath supply to determine how you write. I have had more than one client say to me that they write in short phrases because they run out of air. They do not want to run the risk of an inappropriate pause.

Broadcasters with poor breath support suffer from a number of vocal problems as well. One of the most common is a **glottal fry**. This strange name refers to a popping sound heard toward the ends of sentences when breath supply and pitch drop.

The glottis is the opening between the vocal folds, which is where this sound originates. This condition may have gotten its name because the popping sounds like bacon frying. A glottal fry at the ends of sentences usually indicates that breath supply is low, and pitch is near the bottom of the range. Some speakers like Charles Kuralt and Henry Kissinger have glottal fry elements throughout their speech. Normally, however, the glottal fry will begin a few words before the end of a sentence. Increased air supply and a slight rise in pitch will eliminate a glottal fry as long as it is a functional problem and not organic (see Chapter 2).

Another problem that is common with improper breathing is a very high-pitched voice. When we get nervous or anxious, our pitch generally rises because of increased tension in the throat area. Think of a broadcaster at a noisy political convention or covering a rally. In order to be heard over the crowd, the reporter may talk louder and increase the tension in the throat. What we hear is a higher-pitched voice.

One of my clients who was reporting from the Preakness horse race found she had this problem. When she got in the sound booth to do the narration for the package, she realized she had been shouting over exuberant spectators at the race track. Her pitch in her stand-up had been so high she could not match it in the booth. When the package aired, it sounded like two different reporters because of the differing degrees of vocal tension. With proper breathing, she has now learned how to increase her volume without tensing the laryngeal area.

Tension in the laryngeal area also results from upper chest breathing. The tension it takes to increase the size of the chest cavity using the upper chest muscles can move into the laryngeal area. Chapter 2 describes the way the vocal folds work to vary pitch. Basically, tension causes the folds to become thinner, which produces a higher pitch. If you are breathing in your upper chest, you are increasing the likelihood that your pitch is higher than it should be.

Upper chest breathing may also give you an audible intake of breath. Listeners often complain that they are distracted by the gulps of air they hear reporters taking. That whoosh of air rushing through the mouth can become so predictable it gets in the way of the meaning of the copy.

Taking a good abdominal-diaphragmatic breath before your countdown and another just before you begin your copy will build your air supply (see Breathing Warm-Up 6). This will allow you to take smaller breaths within the copy. It is not possible to take an abdominal-diaphragmatic breath at every pause in your copy. That would be too time-consuming. You have to take short breaths through your mouth when you need air within your copy. When you go to tape for a sound bite or actuality, you may be able to take in another abdominal-diaphragmatic breath. Use every opportunity you have to let the abdominal muscles and the diaphragm do the work.

The Value of Standing for Speech

You will find when doing the Breathing Warm-Ups that standing offers the best posture to fully expand the chest and back area when inhaling. When seated, the abdominal area is pushing up into the dome of the diaphragm. When you stand, the abdominal area is free to expand all around your body. Good singers know this. You rarely see opera singers sing seated. They know that the diaphragm needs freedom to move, and standing allows this.

Most radio studios can accommodate a broadcaster who wants to stand, but many television sound booths are not set up for it. An adjustable mike stand is a small expense, however, when you consider the advantages of standing. CBS has designed a standing desk for Dan Rather, and several other anchors stand even though their desks make them appear seated. They have discovered the advantages of standing.

Some broadcasters have found ingenious ways to free-up the diaphragm. One television network sports announcer who is a former basketball player reportedly kneels in front of the desk in the sound booth. He is well over six feet tall, and kneeling puts him right at mike level. More importantly, it frees the diaphragm by allowing the abdominal area to expand unrestricted.

Another consideration is to avoid the restriction of tight clothing that might keep the abdominal area from expanding. Many broadcasters loosen belts or unbutton waistbands to

A reporter stands as she voices a story.

Courtesy of KGWN–TV, Cheyenne, WY

facilitate easy breathing. Ed Bliss, a former CBS writer, reports
that Allan Jackson, who reported for CBS Radio for over
twenty years, always unbuckled his belt and loosened his pants
after he sat down for a broadcast. You may find you need to do
this, especially if you have just eaten a large meal. Because the
stomach is right below the diaphragm, it is difficult to take a
deep breath with a full stomach.

A reporter demonstrates a sound booth that could be easily adjusted for standing.

Courtesy of WVIR–TV, Charlottesville, VA

Increasing Vocal Energy

A common problem I see with clients is a lack of vocal energy. Some clients sound like they are bored with what they are reporting. They tell me they do not feel that way, but their voice betrays them. This is another problem that can be traced to poor air supply. If you feel bad for some reason, it will most likely be heard in your voice. Our voices often reveal our psychological and physiological states. We have all said to someone, "You don't sound like yourself," or "You sound down." Our voices can signal how we feel, and as a broadcaster you must monitor this.

As a listener or viewer, audience members expect broadcasters to be one step above them in energy level. They want to be convinced that the story they are listening to is important enough to take them away from their everyday lives and into the story. If they are driving, your delivery must be more interesting than the passing scenery. If they are at home or at work, you are competing with an infinite number of distractions. You need to pull your listeners up to your energy level to get them to listen. I often notice that within a news story the people being interviewed sound like they have more energy and involvement than the reporter. This indicates low vocal energy and affects the impact of the story.

Oxygen energizes the mind and body. A good inhalation will not only give you the air you need to speak well, it will also give you the vocal energy you need. You will benefit more from three or four deep abdominal-diaphragmatic breaths than you will from three or four cups of coffee. Yogis have used pranayama, the science of breath control, for centuries to achieve a natural high. Proper breathing can help you achieve the vocal energy needed to pull your listener into your story.

Focus on Breathing

Here is a summary of proper inhalation/exhalation for speech:

Inhalation
1. Diaphragm muscle contracts and flattens downward.
2. Ribs flex upward enlarging the chest cavity.
3. Abdominal area protrudes as diaphragm presses on stomach, liver, and other internal organs.

Exhalation
1. Diaphragm begins to relax.

2. Abdominal muscles control relaxation of diaphragm to create breath support.
3. Ribs slowly move down to relaxed position, and abdominal area returns to normal position.

Before you can begin doing Warm-Ups for Breathing, you must become familiar with the feeling of abdominal-diaphragmatic breathing. The processes described below will help you focus on the muscles involved.

A) Watch a videotape of yourself taking a deep breath. If you are a television broadcaster watch one of your tapes. Otherwise, use a home video recorder to tape yourself reading copy. If a recorder is not available, you may observe yourself in a mirror. Focus on the neck area beneath the chin. Are the muscles of the neck visible when you inhale? Can you see your shoulders move? If either of these is true, you are using your upper chest muscles to inhale.

B) Proper speech production does not begin with the voice being pushed out from the throat or lungs. It begins in the abdominal area. Take a deep breath and sigh. Feel the expansion of the abdomen. Add an audible "ah" sound to the sigh and try to feel the push coming from the abdomen.

C) Various postures and movements force abdominal-diaphragmatic breathing. Try these activities and focus on the movement around the abdominal area, the sides, and the back. Some postures may work better for you than others. In all of them, concentrate on your breathing.

- Bend from the waist at a ninety degree angle, letting your arms and head hang relaxed. Keep your knees slightly flexed. Remain in this position until you can feel your abdominal-diaphragmatic breathing.
- Squat so that your buttocks are resting a few inches above your heels. Remain in this position until you can feel the abdominal involvement in your breathing.

- Sit forward in a chair and put your elbows on your knees. Breathe normally and focus attention on the location of the movement.
- Pant like a dog a dozen times. Slow the panting down and notice the abdomen going out as you inhale and in as you exhale.
- Pretend you are Santa Claus and say a strong, "Ho! Ho! Ho!" several times. Notice that the air is pushed from the abdomen.
- Sit up straight on the front edge of a chair. Drop your arms and grab the legs of the chair to lock your shoulders in place so they cannot rise. Push your abdominal area out as you breathe.
- Take a deep inhalation and pretend you are blowing out one hundred candles on a birthday cake. Feel the pressure in the abdominal area as the muscles squeeze to blow out all the candles.
- Tilt your head back and yawn deeply. Feel the movement in your abdominal area. This is an excellent way to relax the throat.

D) One of the best postures for feeling abdominal-diaphragmatic breathing is lying down. Find a comfortable carpet or bed and stretch out on your back. Spread your legs slightly and move your arms away from your body so that there is open space in your armpits. Perform the following activities:

- Close your eyes and concentrate on your breathing.
- Place your right hand on your chest and your left hand on your abdomen. Notice that you can keep your right hand still while your left hand rises and falls with each breath.
- Keeping your hands on your chest and abdomen, take in a deep inhalation, purse your lips, and blow the air out. Feel your left hand slowly descending as the air is expelled.

- Place a book on your abdomen and watch it rise as you inhale and fall as you exhale.
- Turn over and lie down on your stomach with your hands at your sides. Turn your head sideways and rest your cheek on the bed or floor. Feel your stomach pushing against the surface you are lying on each time you inhale.

E) Working with a partner, put your hand on your partner's abdominal area just above the waist. Ask your partner to inhale and push your hand away. Focus on the movement of the abdominal area. Switch tasks. If either of you has difficulty, forget about breathing and simply push the hand away. Concentrate on moving those muscles, then put an inhalation with the movement.

Breathing Warm-Ups

WARNING: Do not overdo any of the warm-ups in this book. If you feel dizzy or uncomfortable at any time, stop and breathe normally. Do not force or strain.

General Instructions

While doing these warm-ups, use a vocal volume that is appropriate for your broadcast voice or conversation. If the warm-up calls for vocalization, begin the sound immediately. Do not waste any air.

For these warm-ups and for speech, breathing can be done through the mouth. Normally, we breathe through our nose because this filters, warms, and moistens the air. Breathing through the nose is important for normal breathing, but too slow for speech. When speaking, it is appropriate to inhale through the mouth.

These exercises should be done in a standing position. Your posture should be straight, with your knees slightly bent. Try to keep your body as relaxed as possible. As you build your control of exhalation, you will feel the diaphragm rising until it seems to be pushing up into the chest cavity as you reach the end of your vocalization. Do not force vocalization as you deplete your air supply. Always stop if your pitch changes, or if your tone breaks in a glottal fry or a hoarse sound.

You may feel slightly dizzy doing some of these warm-ups. This is especially true if you are a smoker. Deep abdominal-diaphragmatic inhalations bring large supplies of oxygen to your brain. If your body is not accustomed to this, dizziness may occur. If you become dizzy, sit down and breathe normally for a few seconds. As you continue doing these warm-ups, the dizziness should subside. If it does not, see your physician.

Do not worry about hyperventilating during these warm-ups. Hyperventilation is fast, shallow breathing that gives a feeling of breathlessness. It is usually associated with anxiety. Hyperventilation causes the carbon dioxide level to drop and lightheadedness, dizziness, or a giddy feeling results. For these exercises, you will be doing the opposite of hyperventilating. You will be breathing slowly, deeply, and with control. Training in controlled breathing is the common treatment for hyperventilation.

You should make these warm-ups part of your daily routine. Practice at least ten minutes a day for several weeks to build breath support. Select the warm-ups you enjoy for your regular routine and add others for variety. You should also begin to use proper breathing whenever you read copy. Using proper breathing will become a habit if you stay aware of your breathing.

1) This is a negative contrast exercise. Take a deep inhalation in the upper chest area. Exaggerate the lifting of the shoulders and tension in the throat. Say an extended "ah" sound. Time the number of seconds you can sustain an "ah." Listen to the quality of the sound. Next take a comfortable abdominal-diaphragmatic breath in a standing position. If you have difficulty with this, go back to the Focus on Breathing section. Once you have inhaled comfortably with the diaphragm, exhale vocalizing

"ah." Again, time your "ah" and listen to the quality. With the abdominal-diaphragmatic breath, your "ah" should sound lower in pitch and vocalization should be longer.

2) Using a child's pinwheel, purse your lips and blow air out making the pinwheel spin. Use your abdominal muscles to sustain a slow, steady spin. Time how long you can make it spin. Try to increase your time as you repeat this exercise.

3) Tear off the corner of a facial tissue. Hold it against a wall with the force of your exhalation. Feel your abdominal area squeezing in as you exhale for as long as possible.

4) With one hand on your abdominal area, take a deep inhalation pushing your hand out. Sustain any of the following vowel sounds on exhalation:

- "ah" as in spa
- "aw" as in caw
- "u" as in two

Time each vowel production. Stop vocalization when the sound begins to waver or sound weak. At first, your times may be in the ten to fifteen second range. Try to build your control of exhalation by adding a few seconds each time until you can sustain a vowel for twenty to thirty seconds. Keep a record of your progress.

5) Grasp your body so that your fingers touch in the front of your abdominal area and your thumbs reach around toward your back. Take a deep inhalation that pushes your fingers apart. With that breath, vocalize any of the following lists. Make certain that you do not take in any additional small gulps of air. You should be measuring your breath support by exhaling only one inhalation. Keep a record of how far you go each time.

- Repeat the days of the week.
- Count by ones or tens.

- Repeat the months of the year.
- Say the alphabet.

6) This exercise is called the "Countdown to Calm Down." If you practice this enough, it will relieve some of the tension that precedes each taping. Establish a habit of using it in the sound booth or for stand-ups. It will break the tension of the day and get you ready to record.

Take a deep abdominal-diaphragmatic inhalation and say, "Broadcast Voice Handbook story, take one." (You would replace this title with your story slug as you make this part of your routine when you begin recording.) Now inhale deeply again, and say, "Three, two, one." Inhale a third time and begin your story. For a practice story opener you can say, "Broadcasters are finding that a few simple breathing exercises can make a difference."

This method of beginning your taping may seem too slow or time-consuming at first. I have found with clients, however, that the four or five seconds needed for the additional breathing are well worth it. Many clients report that they do fewer takes of each piece with this method. They often are pleased with their voice in the first reading after using their countdown time to calm down.

Correct beginning hand position before and after exhalation.

Courtesy of WVIR–TV, Charlottesville, VA

Correct hand position after abdominal-diaphragmatic inhalation.

Courtesy of WVIR–TV, Charlottesville, VA

7) Take a deep abdominal-diaphragmatic inhalation and say, "Good evening, I'm (your name) and this is Eyewitness News." Exhale any remaining air. Inhale again and say the phrase twice. Continue building the number of times you can repeat the phrase on one inhalation, maintaining an appropriate pitch and volume. Keep a record of your progress.

8) Take a good inhalation and read as far as you comfortably can in the following copy. Meaning is not important. Do not try to "sound like a broadcaster." Mark your progress and try to add one more word each time. Avoid dropping into a glottal fry or forcing. If you find it is easy to read the entire selection in one breath, start over and read until you run out of air.

> A medical researcher says anyone
> who drinks five cups of coffee a
> day, or more, may be increasing the
> chances of developing lung cancer.
> The University of Minnesota
> scientist says his study is the first
> to implicate coffee by itself. He
> also says that if someone drinks
> too much coffee and smokes, the
> combined effects may be far worse.
> But he says investigators must do
> more research.

Reprinted with permission from *Writing Broadcast News*, Mervin Block, Bonus Books, Inc., 1987.

9) Marking your copy for breath pauses will make it easier to avoid inappropriate pauses. In Chapter 5, breath pauses are explained as an integral part of the process of marking copy to add stress and intonation to your reading. For practice purposes, the following selections have been marked for pauses. There are many different ways copy can be marked, and this marking may seem awkward to you. Record these anyway to practice, beginning each with your countdown as in Warm-Up 6. The double slash marks indicate a pause with a fairly deep

inhalation. The single slash marks mean a quick intake of air (called a catch-breath) or a pause with no breath intake.

```
Former President Carter arrived in
New York City today to lend a hand--
/in fact, both of them--/to help
rebuild a burned-out apartment
building.// He came by bus with
other volunteers from his hometown
Baptist church in Plains,
Georgia.// On arrival,/ they talked
over their one-week project,
sponsored by a religious group.//
At the abandoned building on
Manhattan's Lower East Side,/
Mister Carter,/ an expert
woodworker,/ is going to use hammer
and saw to try to make the place fit
again.//


Seven persons in Wilmington,
Delaware, have pointed to a man in
court and identified him as the
bandit who held them up,/ a Roman
Catholic priest.// But now another
man has come forward, saying that
he committed the armed robberies,/
not the priest.// The judge will
decide how to proceed after
conferring today with the
prosecutor,/ the priest/ and the
penitent.//
```

Reprinted with permission from *Writing Broadcast News*, Mervin Block, Bonus Books, Inc., 1987.

10) Try marking the following selections for breath pauses. As you found in Warm-Up 9, most double slash marks are found at periods, and single slashes are at commas, ellipses, dashes, or to distinguish meaning. Once these are marked, continue the reading process you established in Warm-Up 9.

Oregon police are searching for a
prison escapee who was on board the
United Airlines DC-8 that crash-
landed in Portland last night. The
escapee was being returned by two
guards to the Oregon State Prison.
185 persons were on board the
plane. In the crash, at least 10
were killed and 45 hurt, five
critically. And the escapee
apparently escaped again.

Tornadoes and thunderstorms
struck the southeast today and
caused at least two deaths.
Tornadoes in Laurel County,
Kentucky, in the London area,
overturned mobile homes, toppled
trees, battered buildings, peeled
off roofs, killed cattle and
destroyed or damaged a lot of other
property. At least six people there
were hurt.

A fire swept through one of the
nation's biggest libraries today.
The Central Los Angeles Library was
damaged severely, and thousands of
books were destroyed. 250 firemen
fought the fire, and 22 of them were
hurt. Firemen were hampered because
they tried to hold down the use of
water--to minimize water damage to
books.

Reprinted with permission from *Writing Broadcast News*, Mervin Block, Bonus
Books, Inc., 1987.

*Don't ignore voice impairing illnesses. . ..
I have found that most radio news people
don't realize how fragile their voices can be,
until they lose their voice. The recovery time
is typically much longer than expected.*

**Carolynn Jones
News Director, WOBM-FM/AM
Toms River, New Jersey**

*Too often I get air checks from people
who are forcing their voices beyond their
natural ranges.*

**Diane Kepley
News Director, Satellite Music Network
Mokena, Illinois**

*Too many people try to lower their voice
pitch and end up with a loud monotone.
One of the more difficult tasks I've
encountered in this profession is that of
instilling confidence in basic voice quality so
that people can then learn to use what they
have to best effect.*

**Doug Ross
News Director, KPRC
Houston, Texas**

Phonation— Using the Vocal Folds Effectively

Whether you are making $9,000 a year as a general assignment reporter in a small market or $3 million as a network anchor, healthy vocal folds (vocal cords) are a prerequisite to your work. It would be ludicrous to think of a concert pianist laying bricks several hours a week. Obviously, most pianists take very good care of their hands. As a broadcaster, you should be equally protective of your vocal mechanism. If you are misusing your voice, you are playing Russian roulette with the part of your anatomy you must depend on for a lifelong career.

This chapter will explain how talking while you are hoarse, coughing, clearing your throat, and shouting can cause physical damage to your vocal folds. More serious damage is caused by smoking, which remains a career and health hazard for broadcasters.

Anatomy of Phonation

Breathing is your best ally as a broadcaster. It provides the energy for speech while relaxing the body. But breathing alone cannot produce speech. In order for sound to be produced, the air from the lungs must be altered to create sound waves. This is called **phonation**. When we speak, we alter air in several ways, but the most important alteration involves the vocal folds.

The vocal folds are folds of muscle that are located within your larynx (Adam's apple). Their position varies from a fully open V-formation that allows air to flow through unimpeded, to a closed position formed when the sides of the V come together to create a valve in our throats (see Figure 4). This valving is the primary purpose of the vocal folds, not speech. The vocal folds protect our lungs from foreign matter by closing off the trachea when food or liquid comes down the pharynx (see Figure 1). Since the pharynx splits into two tubes—the trachea, that goes to the lungs, and the esophagus, that goes to the stomach—this valve is very important. Without the vocal folds, our lungs would be unprotected, and food and liquid could go into our lungs when we swallow, resulting in asphyxiation. Our vocal folds keep us alive by protecting our lungs.

It is easy to feel your vocal folds working. Slide your fingers down the front of your neck until you reach your larynx, which will feel like a protrusion directly beneath your chin. You are feeling the thyroid cartilage, which is a shield-like structure that protects the vocal folds. With your fingers on your larynx make a sustained "e" sound, and you will feel vibrations. Swallow and feel the larynx rising up in the throat. Yawn and you will feel the larynx moving downward. All of this movement is controlled by an intricate system of muscles in your throat.

The entire structure of the larynx or voice box is an alteration of the top two cartilage rings of the trachea (see Figure 1). These rings have altered to protect the vocal folds and to allow them to open and close. The vocal folds are delicate tissues covered with mucous (see Figure 4). Of all our vocal mechanisms, these structures are the most delicate and the most vulnerable.

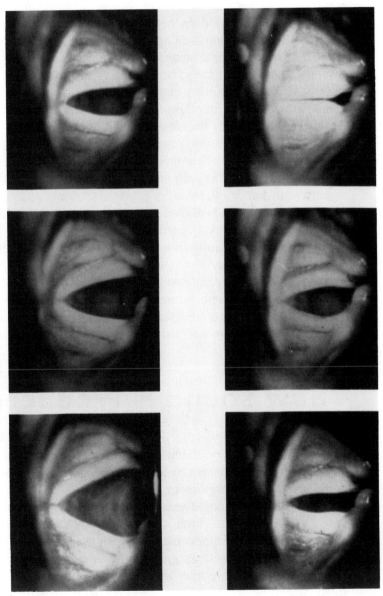

Figure 4
High Speed Photography of Human Vocal Folds Progressing from
Inhalation (upper left) to Voicing (lower right)

Courtesy of AT & T Archives

Most mammals have similar valve systems in their throats to protect their lungs. Other animals' brains and oral structures are not refined enough, however, to produce speech. Cats can meow and dogs bark, but our speech is far more intricate than anything even apes or chimpanzees can produce.

The larynx is arranged in some animals so that they can swallow and smell at the same time to protect themselves while eating. Humans have lost that ability. We cannot inhale while swallowing because our lungs are completely sealed off as a protective measure by the closure of the vocal folds.

We share an important laryngeal attribute with other mammals, however. This is called the glottal effort closure reflex. To feel this reflex, put your palms together and push hard against your hands. To build up pressure to push, you probably closed your vocal folds and trapped air in your lungs. This gives you more upper body strength than you would have with an open airway. Push your hands together and continue breathing as you are pushing, and you will feel much less power.

The primary purposes of the vocal folds are to give us the upper body strength we need and to protect the lungs from foreign matter. When we speak, we are using a life support function that we have adapted to another use.

How Sound Is Produced

To produce sound, we exhale air from the lungs. The brain signals the vocal folds, which are open for normal breathing, to come together to prepare to produce sound. The air builds pressure under the closed vocal folds. When appropriate pressure has built up, the folds are pushed apart. They are then sucked together to block the air again (see Figure 4). This process continues and produces a fluttering effect that alternately blocks the air and lets it pass. This causes the air molecules to be condensed and rarefied, which creates a sound wave. The sound wave can be heard when the altered movement of air forces our eardrum to move at the same frequency as the sound wave.

To experience a process similar to phonation, blow up a balloon and stretch the mouth of the balloon. The air pressure from the balloon will cause the latex at the stretched mouth to flutter, producing a high-pitched squeak. This is caused by the latex being alternately sucked together and pushed apart. Your vocal folds operate much like the mouth of the balloon as they are pulled together and pushed apart to produce sound waves.

Sound waves produced at the vocal folds are measured in cycles per second (cps). A cycle is a complete opening and closing of the vocal folds. Middle C, for example, is 256 cps. These delicate tissues move very rapidly for speech and are vulnerable to misuse.

Common Vocal Problems

To produce sound, the vocal folds must be able to come together as a valve. All the problems associated with phonation involve alteration of the folds, which prevents them from closing effectively. The problems range from a fairly innocuous sore throat to laryngeal cancer. Fortunately, the voice lets us know fairly quickly if there is something wrong in the throat. Pain, hoarseness, and a persistent feeling of a lump in the throat are all signs of a problem.

Hoarseness

The most obvious symptom of a vocal problem is usually hoarseness. It may result from something as simple as a common cold. Hoarseness sounds like a rough, husky, coarse voice. The voice may be lower in pitch than normal and may crack or break as you speak. Any swelling, thickening, or growth on the vocal folds can produce a hoarse voice. Think again of the mouth of a balloon being stretched tightly together. If the latex has a bump in it or is thickened, the closure cannot take place. This is what happens when the folds are swollen or a growth exists.

It is impossible to tell from the sound of your voice whether your hoarseness is caused by a simple swelling, or a benign (noncancerous) or cancerous growth. This is why one of the seven warning symptoms of the American Cancer Society is a nagging cough or hoarseness. In general, if you are hoarse for more than two weeks you should see a doctor. Using a procedure called indirect laryngoscopy, an ear, nose, and throat doctor can look at your vocal folds by inserting something similar to a dentist's mirror in the back of your mouth. Looking down at your folds, the doctor can see what is preventing proper closure.

Laryngitis

A common cause of hoarseness is laryngitis, which in most cases is an acute infection that may be accompanied by a sore throat and fever. This infection usually does not last long, and once the virus is gone your voice returns to normal. Laryngitis changes the healthy pink-colored vocal folds to swollen red tissues.

Chronic laryngitis is a more complex condition caused by vocal misuse. Repeated bouts of laryngitis unaccompanied by fever or sore throat may indicate continued misuse of the vocal mechanism. If your hoarseness is usually worse in the morning when you get up, and you cough frequently, you may suffer from chronic laryngitis. This type of laryngitis requires work with a speech professional to change vocal habits.

In either type of laryngitis the worst thing to do is to continue trying to talk as usual. It is very easy to damage the vocal folds when the tissues are reddened and swollen as they are with laryngitis. When you are hoarse, you should talk as little as possible.

Continuing to talk while hoarse creates what has often been called the *Vicious Circle of Vocal Abuse.* You are hoarse, so you try even harder to talk, which makes you even hoarser, and on and on. Not many of us would run a marathon with tight shoes and continue running the next day despite the blisters and callouses that had developed. All too many broadcasters, however, insist they can go on the air with a hoarse voice. By doing so, they are damaging their vocal folds in the same way you would damage your feet by running when they are red and swollen. Hoarseness should be taken very seriously. Talking while you are hoarse can have long-lasting effects and may cause permanent damage.

Vocal rest is the best treatment for laryngitis. If you must talk, use a breathy voice, not a whisper (see Focus on Phonation). For whispering, the vocal folds are held tightly together and sound is produced through a limited opening. This forces the swollen tissue to be held tightly, causing more abrasion. As an example of a breathy voice, think about a sexy voice like that of Marilyn Monroe, Bo Derek, or Zsa Zsa Gabor. The vocal folds are held open and relaxed, and air comes through the folds without closure of the folds.

If you become hoarse, you can depend on having to rest your voice. It is much healthier for your throat to take time off when you first become hoarse, rather than allowing the condition to get worse through the *Vicious Circle of Vocal Abuse* over several days. It is like the old saying, pay me now or pay me later. At some point, you are going to have to rest your throat. Since the vocal folds are so important to your career, I suggest you take time off and rest when you first feel hoarseness developing.

If you must work while you are hoarse, you should limit your talking. If you are a radio news person and must do hourly spot news, try to remain silent between your broadcasts. Get an assistant to make phone calls for you and to go out in the field. Also limit your talking when you are not at work. All of this will help, but if at all possible, take a day off to rest your voice completely.

Take hoarseness seriously. Remember that you are dealing with two delicate pieces of tissue, and abuse of these tissues can cause permanent damage to your body and your career. I have heard incredible stories from clients about bad advice they have been given. One client said that he was not only encouraged to go on the air when hoarse, but was told that shouting with a hoarse voice would lower his pitch. Bad advice like that could easily end his career as a broadcaster. Having healthy vocal folds should be your top priority, and hoarseness is always a sign that your voice is not working correctly.

Vocal Nodules and Polyps

Continued misuse of your voice when you are hoarse may result in vocal nodules (nodes). If swelling is present in the larynx, as it would be with laryngitis, a thickening of the tissue may occur. If you continue to talk, small wart-like growths the size of a pinhead can develop. These nodules are generally on both sides of the vocal folds (bilateral) and are often directly opposite each other (see Figure 5). The nodules may continue to enlarge, and if vocal abuse continues, speech production may become very difficult.

The vocal symptoms for nodules are similar to laryngitis. The voice is hoarse, low-pitched, and may lack sufficient volume. These symptoms do not go away, however, as they would with acute laryngitis.

Nodules are most common in adult women who speak with a tense, loud voice. The typical candidate for vocal nodules is socially aggressive, talks a lot, and is often in tense situations. All of these characteristics are common traits of broadcasters. The voice may have been high-pitched, but it progresses to a low pitch as the nodules get larger. Nodules or nodes are also common in public speakers, singers, and young children (screamer's nodes).

Vocal nodules develop from a combination of overtaxing the voice and incorrect use of the vocal mechanism. Many singers reportedly have numerous operations to remove vocal nodules. Harry Belafonte, for instance, whose singing is characterized by a staccato, explosive use of the voice, reportedly had such surgery. This type of vocal production is called glottal attack, and results from an intense build-up of air under the closed vocal folds that is allowed to explode out, causing trauma to the tissues.

Vocal polyps are similar to nodules (see Figure 5), but they are usually only on one fold (unilateral). The vocal symptoms of hoarseness and low pitch are the same as for nodules. Unlike nodules, however, vocal polyps may occur from a single traumatic vocal event. This is why it is so important not to scream at a football game or yell across the newsroom. Even an overly vigorous cough or a forceful clearing of your throat can cause a polyp. One loud burst of sound can abuse the vocal folds enough to cause hemorrhaging. Fluid fills the sac caused by the hemorrhage, which produces a polyp.

When broadcasting, remember that an increase in volume may be harmful to your vocal folds. Talk at a conversational level when on-air. The microphone is only a few inches from your mouth, and that should be your point of focus for your volume. There is usually no need to talk louder even in very noisy conditions.

Contact Ulcers

Another benign lesion that can develop on the vocal folds is a contact ulcer. This condition is caused by using a tense voice that has a hard glottal attack. The muscular tension used for this type of voice causes the cartilage near the vocal folds to create an ulcer.

Contact ulcers are most often found in hard-driving middle-aged men. Their voices usually begin as low-pitched with some glottal fry sounds. Broadcasters who lower their pitch unnaturally are good candidates for contact ulcers.

Unlike vocal nodules or polyps, contact ulcers usually cause pain in the throat, neck, or even in the ears during swallowing. The person may feel a tickle or lump in the throat. The voice may progress from being strong and forceful to breathy. The breathy voice is used after the ulcers are present to avoid the pain from forceful closure of the vocal folds.

Contact ulcers may be aggravated by gastrointestinal problems. A condition called gastric reflux may aggravate the ulcers in the larynx. **Gastric reflux** occurs when liquid comes up from the stomach during sleep. This liquid may enter the

Figure 5

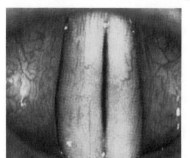

Normal vocal folds (white structures) seen during sound production. Note that healthy vocal folds have a pearly white color and sharp, well-defined contacting surfaces.

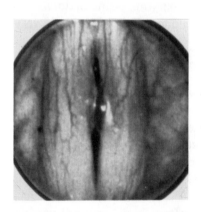

Vocal nodules on both vocal folds. These lesions result from vocal abuse and cause incomplete closure, irregular margins and added mass to the vocal folds. These contribute to breathiness, hoarseness, lowered pitch and sometimes roughness in the voice.

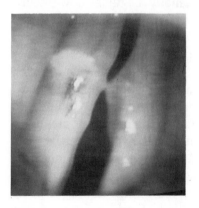

Vocal fold polyp (right) resulting from vocal abuse in an 18-year-old acting student. Note the irregularities and swelling in the mucosa on the non-lesioned (left) vocal fold.

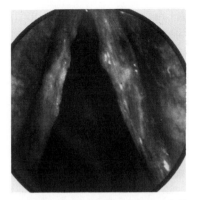 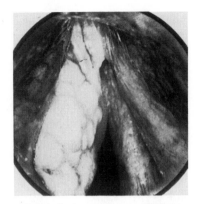

Two laryngoscopic views of the vocal folds in long term smokers. Note that this habit can result in inflammation, architectural changes and the possible development of cancerous lesions on the vocal folds.

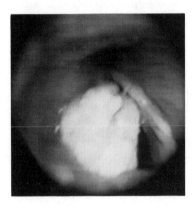

Laryngoscopic view of a large benign tumor of the vocal fold (cottonball structure) found in a 28-year-old woman who was first examined after experiencing hoarseness for three months. This case emphasizes the need to receive medical evaluation of hoarseness that persists for longer than 2 weeks.

Figures provided with the compliments of the Memphis Voice Care Center, a comprehensive multidisciplinary medical specialty clinic dedicated solely to the care of voice and voice-related problems. Through medical treatment, long-range vocal management planning, and continued vocal education, the Center helps patients keep their voices in top shape.

pharynx and move into the laryngeal area, causing irritation to the vocal folds. Avoid heavy evening meals, and do not eat at least two hours before going to sleep to avoid gastric reflux.

Treatment for Vocal Nodules, Polyps, and Ulcers

The good news about all of the benign conditions described above is that they may not require surgery, and they do not appear to be pre-malignant conditions. They are caused by vocal misuse; when the misuse goes away so does the condition. New diagnostic procedures and equipment as well as research have shown that most of these conditions will completely disappear when the voice is used correctly.

Dr. Joshua Oppenheim, an ear, nose, and throat specialist (otolaryngologist) in the Washington, D.C., area, reports that 90 percent of his patients with nodules, polyps, or ulcers do not require surgery. Often, though, work with a speech pathologist to learn proper vocal production is necessary. This work might last from six months to a year in some cases, and involves reducing tension in the larynx and learning to talk with a relaxed voice. Medical treatment is often necessary to control gastric reflux.

If you remain hoarse for more than two weeks, the first step is to get a proper diagnosis. An otolaryngologist might use indirect laryngoscopy or a newer technique called videostroboscopy. This technique involves the use of a video camera and a strobe light. By projecting the strobe light down the throat and timing its flash, the video camera shows the vibrations of the vocal folds as a wave-like movement. This technique allows physicians to view the size and type of the vocal fold problem as well as the resulting interruption in the vibration. Dr. Oppenheim has observed that this equipment allows for a much more precise diagnosis.

If you are having vocal problems, seek a specialist with the latest equipment. Also, always get a second opinion if you are advised to have surgery to remove a benign lesion. In the past, surgery was often recommended, but, as has been pointed out, it may be unnecessary or inappropriate. Surgery is still required in some instances to cure vocal fold lesions that do not respond well to medical or speech therapy, but a second opinion is always appropriate.

Cancer of the Larynx

All vocal problems are not as easily treated as nodules, polyps, and ulcers. Laryngeal cancer requires surgery or radiation, and is a life-threatening condition. The American Cancer Society reports that laryngeal cancer strikes approximately 12,000 persons in the United States each year and causes 3,800 deaths.

As with the benign conditions described above, hoarseness is usually the first symptom of laryngeal cancer, which most often begins as a growth on the vocal folds (see Figure 5). Other symptoms may be a change in pitch, a sense of discomfort or lump in the throat, coughing, difficulty or pain in breathing or swallowing, and earache. Since these symptoms can also signal benign conditions, it is important to have them diagnosed by a physician if they persist for more than two weeks.

The impact of laryngeal cancer on a broadcaster's voice can be profound. Even the nonsurgical technique of radiation therapy can affect the sound of the voice. Surgery to remove a cancerous growth usually affects vocal production significantly. If a laryngectomy is required, the voice is completely lost when the larynx is removed. Following the surgery, the patient breathes through a tracheostoma, a hole made in the lower front of the neck. This is necessary because the important valve provided by the vocal folds has been removed, and the path to the lungs is unprotected. During the surgery it is necessary to block off the trachea permanently from the mouth, and channel breathing out the tracheostoma. In addition to losing the capability of normal vocal production, laryngectomy patients are also physically weaker because they no longer have the glottal effort closure reflex explained earlier in this chapter.

Smoking and Cancer

Unlike nodules, polyps, or ulcers, laryngeal cancer is not caused from vocal misuse. The most common cause of laryngeal cancer is cigarette smoking (see Figure 5). In fact, the American Cancer Society reports that almost all those who develop cancer of the larynx use or have used tobacco. Cigarettes have chemicals that directly irritate the vocal folds when being inhaled and exhaled. Alcohol consumption is another important risk factor. People who smoke *and* drink are at highest risk of cancer.

In addition, smoking is the primary factor in oral cancer which, like laryngeal cancer, can have devastating effects on a broadcaster. According to the American Cancer Society, oral cancer strikes approximately 30,500 persons in the United States each year, causing 8,350 deaths. The death rate from oral cancer is about four times higher for smokers than for nonsmokers. Pipe and cigar smokers may develop oral cancer even if they do not inhale smoke into their lungs.

If those cancers are not enough reason to avoid smoking, lung cancer should be. Smoking has been shown to have a direct connection to lung cancer. The American Cancer Society says that smoking is responsible for 83 percent of lung cancers. They expect 157,000 new cases in 1990 and 142,000 deaths. A person who smokes two packs a day is twenty-five times more likely to die of lung cancer than a nonsmoker.

The dangers of smoking are not limited to broadcasters who smoke. Involuntary smoking (inhaling smoke from someone else's cigarette) is estimated to cause nearly 2 percent of the annual lung cancer deaths per year (National Academy of Sciences report quoted by the American Cancer Society). This amounts to 2,400 persons who die from lung cancer caused from others' cigarettes. The American Cancer Society has found that nonsmokers exposed to twenty or more cigarettes a day at home or work had twice the risk of developing lung cancer. In addition, involuntary smokers suffer more colds, bronchitis, chronic coughs, and ear infections, and have reduced lung function.

To summarize the devastating effects of smoking, the American Cancer Society reports in its "Cancer Facts and Figures" for 1990 that cigarette smoking is the single main cause of cancer mortality in the United States. Smoking is directly related to 1,068 deaths *per day* in this country. Compare this to scheduled airline flight fatalities, which totalled only 285 *per year* for 1988 (reported by the National Transportation Safety Board), and you begin to understand the significance.

When I speak to groups of broadcasters, I tell them that smoking is just plain stupid if you value your career and your life. The evidence is overwhelming and irrefutable. It is not even a good gamble. If you smoke, the odds are that you will develop vocal problems. Why spend years training to be the best broadcaster you can be, only to defeat yourself by smoking?

Do not admire the classic "smoker's voice." Smokers generally do have a lower-pitched voice, but that is because of the trauma smoking causes to the vocal folds. Incredibly, I was told of a news director who advised the women in his shop to smoke because it would lower their pitch. That advice is the equivalent of telling someone to drive while drunk because he or she will be more relaxed. The effects can be deadly.

Remember the danger of involuntary smoking as well. Campaign for a smokeless newsroom. We now have smoke-free airline flights, offices, and restaurants. CNN company policy prohibits smoking in all its newsrooms. Insist on the same for your newsroom.

The once common image of the smoke-filled newsroom should be history. Far too many broadcasters, including Edward R. Murrow, have died from smoking-related illnesses. Ed Bliss, Murrow's writer at CBS Radio, reports that Murrow smoked three to four packs of unfiltered Camels a day. A former Murrow writer advised Bliss to never use adjectives in his copy and always carry a fresh pack of Camels for Murrow. Murrow died of lung cancer at the age of 57. All the facts about smoking that are now common knowledge were not available thirty years ago. Broadcasters today should avoid all contact with tobacco smoke.

Taking Care of Your Voice

In addition to avoiding tobacco smoke, there are other steps you can take to have a healthy voice. Luckily, vocal hygiene and basic good health often go hand in hand.

Coughing

Straining the voice in any way has a harmful effect on the vocal folds. Perhaps the most common vocal abuse is coughing. When we cough, we build up tremendous air pressure under the vocal folds. The air moves up the trachea very rapidly after being forcefully exhaled by a push from the abdominal muscles. This blast of air is intended to blow any obstruction out of our throat. This might be mucous, if we have a cold, or a piece of food that has started down toward the laryngeal area. When we cough, the air leaving the lungs is moving at close to supersonic speeds. The folds vibrate explosively, which is what is needed to clear the throat.

The force that makes a cough work may also damage the delicate throat tissue. Excessive coughing can be harmful to the vocal folds because of the forceful closure it causes. The folds may begin to swell and eventually become thickened. Any cold or allergy should be controlled to limit the need for coughing.

In certain instances, a blast of air similar to that of a cough can save a person's life. The Heimlich Maneuver (taught by the American Red Cross and the American Heart Association as part of CPR instruction) involves forcing air through the trachea to dislodge food or objects totally blocking the trachea. When foreign matter is caught in the vocal folds, the person cannot make a sound. The universal sign for choking is to grab the throat area. A person is unable to cough, speak, or breathe. During the Heimlich Maneuver, the person's abdominal area is compressed forcefully. The diaphragm rises, and the effect is as if you slammed the handles of a bellows closed. Anything stuck in the tube of the bellows would be blasted out. In a similar manner, food stuck in someone's throat may actually fly across the room if the Heimlich Maneuver is done correctly.

Throat Clearing

Throat clearing can also be harmful if done excessively. As when coughing, clearing your throat causes your folds to vibrate explosively. This can cause swelling and may lead to the development of polyps or nodules on the vocal folds. Clearing your throat is like a small cough, and it can become a habit. Some people feel the need to clear their throat repeatedly through the day. Try to be aware of how often you clear your throat and keep it to a minimum. You may have to ask a friend to observe how many times you clear your throat, since this action is often unconscious.

Allergies are often a factor in throat clearing. If you find yourself clearing your throat a great deal, it might be helpful to have yourself tested for different allergies. An allergy to certain foods or substances may be causing your discomfort.

One food group that commonly makes people clear their throats and cough is milk products. If you like to drink milk in the morning or have cereal for breakfast, you may find yourself clearing your throat all morning. Milk products establish a condition in our throats conducive to the development of mucous. If you avoid milk products before going on air, you will find your throat much clearer. Save the consumption of milk products for after your on-air work if you find they contribute to coughing or throat clearing.

Loud Speech

Vocal nodules and polyps are linked with overly loud speech. For loud speech, the vocal folds come together very forcefully. They open slower but close much more quickly.

Most broadcasters are aware of their volume on the air because of the advice they receive from engineers. What they may not monitor, however, is the volume of their speech at other times. Many people with slight hearing loss, for instance, consistently speak too loudly.

Newsroom noise may contribute to loud speech.

Courtesy of KLS-TV, Salt Lake City, UT

Another condition that may cause loud speech is a noisy newsroom without an intercom. All too often I find myself in a newsroom where the wire service machines are running, several monitors are on, and ten or twenty people are trying to talk on the phone or to others in the newsroom. As calls come in, I hear on-air broadcasters shouting over this chaos to tell someone else to pick up the phone.

For good vocal hygiene, you should limit your talking in noisy places. This includes the newsroom described above as well as cars or vans, airplanes, trains, or anywhere that requires an increase in volume. And, of course, avoid shouting at sports or music events. Remember that you are making your living on those two little muscles in your throat, and you must take care of them.

Vocal Hydration

The vocal folds are covered with mucous. This moist condition is important to aid in proper vocal fold closure. If the throat is dry, the folds are more likely to be damaged because they lack

Often reporters' assignments require broadcasting from noisy locations such as Dan Rather faced in Tiananmen Square during the China uprising, May 1989.

Courtesy of CBS News.

the appropriate mucous to protect them. Any condition that dehydrates body tissues also drys out the throat.

Excessive mouth breathing can dry out the throat. It is appropriate to breathe through your mouth when you are talking. At other times, breathing should be through the nose so that the air can be filtered, warmed, and moisturized before it goes into the laryngeal area. If you have any blockage in the nose that causes mouth breathing, it should be corrected. In addition, you should avoid breathing through your mouth when you are asleep. Sleeping on your back will often cause mouth breathing. Since this sleeping posture may cause back pain as well, it should be avoided. Sleeping on your side with your mouth closed is best.

If you have a cold or a stuffy nose, decongestants will help open a blocked nasal cavity, but they accomplish this by drying out the tissues. If the nose is dried out, the throat is also.

When you have a cold it is difficult to avoid drying the throat, since you will most likely be breathing through your mouth if you do not take a decongestant. This is one of the reasons why it is so important to drink plenty of liquids and inhale steam when you have cold symptoms.

Forced air heating and air conditioning are used in most homes and newsrooms as well as on airplanes and trains. This dry air also contributes to a dry throat. If you live and work in this type of environment or in an excessively dry climate, a humidifier should be used. This pumps moisture into the air to lessen the harmful drying effects of the forced air. You can also inhale moisture by using a facial steamer, which gives you the added advantage of moisturizing your facial tissues as well. Simply inhaling steam from a pot of boiling water will also help your throat. (Make certain it does not burn your throat or skin.)

One important chemical that takes water out of the body by acting as a diuretic on the kidneys is caffeine (or technically xanthine, which includes the chemicals in tea and cocoa). One cup of coffee will not have a tremendous effect on your tissues, but if you combine that with other sources of caffeine (see Table 1), you can easily suffer from its usage.

It is easy for caffeine consumption to become excessive. Looking at Table 1, you will see that if you consumed three cups of coffee, a glass of iced tea, an ounce of chocolate, a Diet Coke, and two Excedrin tablets in one day you would be in the range of 610 milligrams of caffeine. Since caffeine also stimulates the central nervous system and your heart, excessive amounts are not good for your throat or your body. Most recommendations suggest no more than two cups of coffee a day or around 200 milligrams. Caffeine does give you a sense of alertness, but as Chapter 1 explained, that can be achieved in healthier ways through proper breathing.

Alcohol also works as a diuretic. It robs your tissues of needed moisture. Dehydration may be the cause of the hangover headache. The classic symptoms of dry mouth and excessive thirst the morning after signal the degree of dehydration that has occurred. In addition, chronic alcohol abuse is linked with laryngeal and oral cancer. For a healthy body and voice, alcohol consumption should be limited.

Table 1
Caffeine Content of Beverages, Foods, and Common Drugs

	Milligrams of Caffeine
Coffee (5 oz.)	
Brewed, drip method	115
Brewed, percolator	80
Instant	65
Decaffeinated, brewed	3
Decaffeinated, instant	2
Tea (5 oz.)	
Brewed, major U.S. brands	40
Brewed, imported brands	60
Instant	30
Iced (12 oz.)	70
Cocoa beverage (5 oz.)	4
Chocolate milk beverage (8 oz.)	5
Milk chocolate (1 oz.)	6
Dark chocolate, semisweet (1 oz.)	20
Baker's chocolate (1 oz.)	26
Chocolate-flavored syrup (1 oz.)	4

Source: FDA, Food Additive Chemistry Evaluation Branch, based on evaluations of existing literature on caffeine levels.

Soft Drinks (12 oz.)	
Sugar-Free Mr. PIBB	58.8
Mountain Dew	54.0
Mello Yellow	52.8
TAB	46.8
Coca-Cola	45.6
Diet Coke	45.6
Shasta Cola	44.4

	Milligrams of Caffeine
Shasta Cherry Cola	44.4
Shasta Diet Cola	44.4
Mr. PIBB	40.8
Dr. Pepper	39.6
Sugar-Free Dr. Pepper	39.6
Big Red	38.4
Sugar-Free Big Red	38.4
Pepsi-Cola	38.4
Aspen	36.0
Diet Pepsi	36.0
Pepsi Light	36.0
RC Cola	36.0
Diet Rite	36.0
Kick	31.2
Canada Dry Jamaica Cola	30.0
Canada Dry Diet Cola	1.2

Source: Institute of Food Technologists (IFT), April 1983, based on data from the National Soft Drink Association, Washington, D.C. IFT also reports that there are at least 68 flavors and varieties of soft drinks produced by 12 leading bottlers that have no caffeine.

	Milligrams of Caffeine
Prescription Drugs	
Cafergot (for migraine headaches)	100
Fiorinal (for tension headaches)	40
Soma Compound (muscle relaxant)	32
Darvon Compound (pain relief)	32.4
Nonprescription Drugs	
Weight-Control Aids	
Dex-A-Diet II	200
Dexatrim Extra Strength	200
Dietac capsules	200
Maximum Strength Appedrine	100
Prolamine	140
Alertness Tablets	
Nodoz	100
Vivarin	200

Analgesic/Pain Relief	
Anacin, Maximum Strength	
Anacin	32
Excedrin	65
Midol	32.4
Vanquish	33
Diuretics	
Aqua-Ban	100
Maximum Strength Aqua-Ban	
Plus	200
Permathene H2 Off	200
Cold/Allergy Remedies	
Coryban-D capsules	30
Triaminicin tablets	30
Dristan Decongestant tablets &	
Dristan A-F Decongestant	
tablets	16.2
Duradyne-Forte	30

Source: FDA's National Center for Drugs and Biologics. FDA also notes that caffeine is an ingredient in more than 1,000 nonprescription drug products as well as numerous prescription drugs.

The best way to combat the drying effects of alcohol, caffeine, and environmental factors is to drink as much water as possible. A minimum of thirty-two ounces of tepid water a day is recommended. (An effective gauge that doctors often recommend is to always drink enough water to keep your urine clear.) It is much healthier to keep a mug filled with water, rather than coffee, on your desk. Avoid ice water as it may constrict the muscles in your throat.

If you feel the need to drink warm liquids, try to avoid caffeine. You can drink decaffeinated coffee or tea, herbal tea, or warm water with lemon. Singers try spraying their throats with various solutions to increase moisture, but this is not necessary if you drink plenty of liquids. In addition, be aware that gargling may dry and stress the vocal fold area since you are blowing air up forcefully to gargle. The best way to have a healthy, well-hydrated throat is to drink plenty of water.

The Ideal Newsroom

I often joke with news directors that my ideal newsroom would have sound booths set up for standing, a standing anchor desk, no smoking signs everywhere, spring water dispensers instead of coffee pots, intercoms to avoid yelling, and humidifiers. I am not sure I will see every newsroom making these changes in this century, but as more data becomes available about the harmful behaviors mentioned above, changes will occur.

Pitch

We not only produce sound with our vocal folds, but we also have the ability to alter the pitch or musical note of that sound. We alter pitch by increasing or decreasing the vibrations per second of the vocal folds. We can go from middle C (256 cps) to high C (512 cps) and cover all the pitches in between. Sing this eight tone (one octave) scale (do-re-mi-fa-sol-la-ti-do). This is accomplished by a subtle shortening and lengthening of the vocal folds.

The V-shaped opening of the vocal folds is positioned with the folds connecting in the front of our throat. The apex/bottom of the V is directly behind the thyroid cartilage (Adam's apple). The two ends of the folds that move are toward the back of the trachea. They are each connected to a triangular-shaped arytenoid cartilage. These cartilages can pivot, rotate, and tilt backwards or sideways to alter the length of the folds and thus change the pitch.

The pitch we create is determined by the length, thickness, and degree of tension of the folds. Men's voices are generally about one octave lower than women's because men have longer vocal folds (around three-quarters of an inch in men versus one-half inch in women). During childhood, girls and boys have similar pitches. The male larynx, however, goes through an explosion of growth at puberty and nearly doubles in size. During this spurt of growth, boys' voices are very unpredictable, and often produce embarrassing voice breaks.

A healthy voice has a range of about one and one-half octaves. Opera singers expand their range significantly, with men reaching two octaves and women often reaching three. A tenor, for example, might sing from middle C (256 cps) down an octave (128 cps) and up an octave (512 cps). This skill comes from practice and training to expand pitch range.

When we lower our pitch, the arytenoid cartilages move so that the folds become shorter and thicker. Low pitch is produced by short, thick, relaxed folds. For high pitch, the folds are stretched tight, producing thinner, tenser folds. The pitch is determined by the cross-sectional mass. Thick folds move slowly, which produces a low pitch, and thin, tense folds move more rapidly, producing a high pitch.

To achieve this change in pitch, the muscles in the larynx must move. The larynx actually rises in the throat slightly for a high-pitched sound and moves down noticeably for a low pitch. To experience this, put your fingers on your Adam's apple and hum a familiar song such as "Happy Birthday." You will feel the larynx moving as the pitch changes.

It is interesting to watch the head positions of television news reporters and anchors as they change pitch. Many times the head will drop down when the pitch is lowered on a word or phrase. Proponents of the affected "Ted Baxter" voice often lower their chin and compress the neck area before beginning their on-air voice. If you remember Ted on "The Mary Tyler Moore Show," you know that his conversational voice was much higher-pitched than his on-air voice. The Jim Dial character on the show "Murphy Brown" is another good example of this affected voice.

It is important to note that pitch is accomplished by changing the tension in the throat. A higher pitch is produced by greater tension. If you feel your pitch is consistently too high, it may be because of too much tension in the throat. Think of how your voice sounds when you are relaxed and contented, such as when you first awaken or after a cozy evening by the fire. You might say you have a mellow voice. Compare this to your voice in the sound booth after a frantic day of news coverage. You might characterize both your day and your voice as tense. It is this tension that causes the pitch to rise.

If you feel your voice is too high-pitched, the first step toward improving it is to achieve relaxation in the throat area. Most of us hold our greatest degree of tension in our shoulders and neck area. Relaxing this area is imperative for good vocal production. Using abdominal-diaphragmatic breathing will help a great deal (see Focus on Breathing and Breathing Warm-Ups in Chapter 1). Relaxing your neck by doing simple neck rolls will help as well (see Focus on Phonation, Phonation Warm-Ups, and Appendix D). Be aware that a tense body usually means a tense voice.

Optimum Pitch

Inappropriate habitual pitch can cause vocal abuse. If you are speaking above or below your natural frequency, you are using unnecessary muscular energy, which can result in vocal fatigue and hoarseness. Voice professionals disagree about whether inappropriate pitch can cause vocal nodules, but there is evidence to link excessive low pitch to contact ulcers.

Equally as important to you as a broadcaster is the effect of inappropriate pitch on expressiveness. If you are consistently talking at the low end of your pitch range, you have no room to drop your pitch for emphasis. The same is true of a pitch that is too high.

I rarely see clients who feel their pitch is too low. Most clients complain that their voice is too high-pitched. The questionnaire results in Appendix A confirm that news directors agree. Twenty-five percent say high pitch is a problem, and only 13 percent mention low pitch. (Note that radio and television news directors differ on this.) Many times broadcasters adopt an inappropriately low pitch to compensate for a pitch they feel is too high. They drop their pitch when they go on the air. By doing this, they accomplish a low-pitched sound, but the damage they are doing to their vocal folds becomes apparent. They often complain of vocal fatigue, breathiness, or frequent bouts of hoarseness.

The goal for proper voice production is to talk in your optimum pitch range, which is usually around one-fourth of the way up from the bottom of your range. At your optimum pitch, the muscles of the larynx are functioning best, and your voice is comfortable to use. Pitch changes are easy to produce and require the least effort when you are using your optimum pitch. The most resonant tones are produced at the optimum pitch because it matches the pitch range of the resonators above the larynx (see Chapter 3).

It is difficult in a book such as this to give instructions on how to find your optimum pitch range. That is more appropriately done by a voice coach, singing teacher, or speech pathologist. Suffice it to say, however, that achieving relaxation in the vocal mechanism is always the first step toward finding your optimum pitch range.

Problems that are perceived as pitch problems are often not related to phonation, but to resonance, which is the enrichment of the sound in our vocal cavities. You are not the best judge of whether your voice is too high-pitched. I often find that clients are using the correct pitch but are limiting vocal resonance in such a way that their voice seems high-pitched and thin. These clients need work on resonance, not pitch. (For more on resonance, see Chapter 3.)

Beware of anyone who advises you to lower your pitch. As has been noted, finding your best pitch range is a complicated process, and not something with which to experiment. It should only be done with the guidance of a trained professional.

If you came to me as a client and had a fairly high-pitched voice, I could certainly give you a deeper voice by telling you to drop your pitch an octave. Likewise, I could make you seem taller by telling you to walk on your tiptoes all the time. Both of these activities would produce the desired results, but they would do so at the expense of your muscles. Eventually you would not be able to talk or walk without problems.

In lectures to news directors, I often play a tape of a client who came to me because of vocal fatigue. His conversational voice was relaxed and pleasant. As soon as I handed him a microphone, however, he dropped his voice into an unnaturally low pitch. I finally convinced him his natural pitch was appropriate for the air. The before and after tape I play usually brings laughter because he sounds so much better in his natural pitch range. Everyone wonders why he suffered so long to produce a tense, unnatural, low-pitched voice.

Your goal should be to talk in a relaxed, well-resonated voice that requires the least amount of energy to maintain. Manipulating the muscles in your throat to achieve a voice you or others think sounds better can result in vocal damage. You might have a great voice for a few years, but your career will be limited by the strain you are putting on your vocal mechanism.

Focus on Phonation

Here is a summary of the advice given in this chapter to help you have a healthy voice. These recommendations are important to observe daily, and are especially important if you have a cold or sore throat.

Ten Recommendations for a Healthy Voice

1) Practice abdominal-diaphragmatic breathing to decrease tension in the laryngeal area.
2) Do not smoke or expose yourself to the smoke of others.
3) Avoid excessive alcohol consumption.
4) Avoid eating at least two hours before you go to bed. Avoid milk products before on-air work.
5) Do not talk loudly or in noisy environments such as airplanes, cars, boats, or sports and music events.
6) Keep your vocal tract moist by drinking at least 32 ounces of tepid or warm water a day, using a humidifier or inhaling steam, and avoiding substances and environ-

ments that dehydrate. Decaffeinated
warm drinks may also be consumed, or
hot water with lemon.
7) Avoid mouth breathing except for speech.
Limit throat clearing and coughing.
8) If you do become hoarse, limit your
talking, and use a breathy voice, not a
whisper.
9) Use a pitch that is comfortable and does
not cause vocal fatigue.
10) See a physician if hoarseness, pain, or
odd sensations in the throat last for more
than two weeks.

Relaxation is the key to good phonation. Many of the
activities listed below are designed to achieve maximum relaxation in the laryngeal area.

A) A whisper requires a great deal of tension in the
vocal folds. They must come together tightly, and sound is
produced in a small opening. To feel the tension this requires,
imagine you are leading your crew out of a city council meeting.
You must get everyone to follow you to the van, but you do not
want to disturb the meeting. Whisper loudly, "Come with me,
everybody." Whisper this several times and feel the tension in
your throat. Now completely relax your throat and attempt to
say the same phrase in a breathy voice. Begin with a barely
audible sound that feels like the "h" in "hello." For a breathy
voice, the vocal folds are left open in their V-shaped position
and air rushes over them. The throat remains completely
relaxed. The breathy voice will not sound as loud, but the throat
will be relaxed. This is the voice you should use when you have
any hoarseness or discomfort in your throat.

B) For negative contrast, take a breath using the
clavicular muscles, so that the shoulders rise on inhalation.
After you have inhaled, hold the breath and feel the tension in
your throat. Next, take an abdominal-diaphragmatic breath (see
Focus on Breathing in Chapter 1). Hold the breath and compare

the degree of tension in the throat. You should feel much less tension with the abdominal-diaphragmatic breath.

C) To feel the larynx moving, put your fingers on your Adam's apple and make an "e" sound as in "bee." Change the pitch of the sound and feel the larynx rise for the higher pitch and move downward for the lower pitch.

D) To compare voiced and voiceless sounds in our language, put your fingers on your Adam's apple. Bring your lips together and make a "p" sound (the initial sound in the word "pot"). Now make a "b" sound (as in "Bob"). You should feel vibrations of the vocal folds for the "b" but not for the "p."

E) If you want to get a feeling of what your optimum pitch might be, sigh deeply with an "ah" sound. This "ah" will usually be in your optimum pitch.

F) To avoid laryngeal tension, you should develop the sense that your voice does not come from your larynx or your mouth, but from your diaphragm in the solar plexus region. Our entire body produces speech. Imagine a bellows with a reed at the end of the neck. All the energy to make that reed vibrate comes from your arms pushing the bellows shut. The reed does not move by itself. In the same way, our voice does not come from the vocal folds, but begins with the breath, which is the energy that produces the movement of the folds. Gaining a sense of body involvement in vocal production can be helpful in eliminating tension and producing the healthiest voice possible. Two authors who have written extensively on body involvement in speech are Kristin Linklater and Arthur Lessac (see Suggested Readings). Their books are recommended. In addition, instruction in the Alexander Technique, tai chi, and yoga can help develop this feeling. Acting classes are also helpful.

Phonation Warm-Ups

Phonation warm-ups are aimed at reducing tension in the laryngeal area. They should be performed until relaxation has occurred. Be careful not to exercise the vocal folds too much since vocal fatigue may occur.

1) Yawning has been used for centuries as a technique to relax the throat. A good yawn relaxes the larynx and throat and brings in a good air supply. Practice yawning for relaxation. Drop the jaw and think of what a good yawn feels like. Yawning is sometimes contagious, so take the opportunity to yawn when you see others doing so. Add a sigh at the end of your yawn to feel your relaxed, open throat. After yawning, say this phrase with the same open throat, "How many hats does Henry have?" Say this several times, trying to preserve the open feeling.

Most of us tend to hold tension in our shoulders, upper back, and neck. To relieve this tension, try these warm-ups. Be careful not to stretch your muscles too much.

2) Clasp your hands behind your back. Squeeze your shoulder blades together and raise your arms slightly, tilting your head back. Hold your arms up for five seconds at the point you feel resistance. Release. Repeat this warm-up until your shoulders and upper back feel relaxed.

3) Place your hands on your shoulders. Rotate your shoulders by bringing your elbows together in front, moving them down, back, and up in a circular movement. Rotate five times in one direction and five times in the opposite direction.

4) Very slowly drop your chin to your chest and roll your head up to your right shoulder. Roll your head back down to your chest and roll your head up to your left shoulder. Bring your chin back down to your chest. Repeat slowly three times. (Do not roll your head back. This may cause neck injuries.)

5) Look straight ahead. Rotate your head slowly and look over each shoulder as if you were signaling an exaggerated "no." Repeat twice.

6) To relax the throat, take a deep abdominal-diaphragmatic breath and exhale an "ah" sound. Inhale again and exhale an "ou" sound as in "you." Inhale a third time and exhale an "m" sound. Feel the resonance in the nasal cavity for the "m."

7) To gain flexibility in pitch, say "one" at your normal pitch level. Now go up one step in pitch and say "two." Go up another step in pitch and say "three." Go back down to your normal pitch with "three, two, one." Now go down in pitch one step and say "two." Go down another step and say "three." Go back up to your normal pitch. This process would look like this:

```
        three three
   two              two
one              one one                     one
                     two              two
                   three three
```

You might want to trace the steps in pitch in the air with your finger as your voice produces them. Tape recording this and the following warm-up work will help you hear if you are really producing the pitch changes you hope for.

8) Continue pitch work by saying the phrase

```
                 up
"My voice is going      in pitch."
"My voice is going      in pitch."
                 down
```

Repeat these two phrases until you feel comfortable with your pitch changes.

9) Use this phrase to expand your pitch range:

```
                          up."
                      up
                   up
                 up
              up
"I can make my voice go
```

"I can make my voice go

        down

           down

              down

                  down

                      down."

When doing this warm-up, do not push your voice into an artificially high or low pitch. Going too high or low can cause vocal fatigue and possible abuse. For a falsetto, for example, the vocal folds are pulled excessively tight, and they lose their wave-like motion. As with any unnatural position of the folds, this can be harmful.

10) Sing up the musical scale by singing

               do

             ti

            la

          sol

        fa

      mi

    re

  do

Do this until you feel comfortable with these eight tones.

Too much emphasis has been placed on "booming pipes" in radio. Radio announcers should talk like people *talk.*

Lee Hall
News Director, WSB
Atlanta, Georgia

Voice instructors should not *try to improve newscasters by trying to make their voices deeper. Credible, conversational deliveries are much more important than deep voices.*

Dan Shelley
News Manager, KTTS Radio
Springfield, Missouri

It's not always important to have what we in the profession call "deep pipes," if you can read well and express yourself to the viewer or listener. A deep voice is not the key to getting that elusive radio or TV job.

Shedd Johnson
News Director, WRAL-FM &
The North Carolina News Network
Raleigh, North Carolina

Resonance— Enriching Speech Sound

When people criticize the quality of a broadcaster's voice, they are usually talking about resonance. The vocal folds generate sound waves, but the resonating cavities enrich and augment the sound. Just as no two people look exactly alike, no two vocal mechanisms are exactly alike. The difference in the shape, size, and resiliency of the resonating cavities makes each voice unique.

Resonance not only gives us each a different voice, but it also allows our voices to be heard. To create sound waves, the vocal folds set air in motion in a wave-like fashion, bursting open and closed. If these sound waves were not resonated, they would produce a faint sound, barely audible to the human ear. The slight movement of air at the vocal folds must be enriched by the air and resonating structures above it in the throat.

Characteristics of Resonance

All sound-producing instruments use resonance to enrich their sounds. A guitar string nailed between two pieces of wood would not make a musical sound that you could hear easily. Plucking that string would produce a very thin, weak sound. Put that string on a guitar, however, and the sound is enriched by the body of the guitar and the air trapped in the body. The sound waves become louder and richer.

Resonance is the ability of one body of molecules to set another body of molecules into the same wave-like motion. These may be air molecules or a solid structure. Notice how solid objects vibrate when there is a loud crash of thunder or an explosion. If you feel a table or wall when this happens, you can feel the molecules moving (vibrating).

Touching a vibrating tuning fork to different surfaces also demonstrates how solid matter resonates sound. A vibrating middle C tuning fork will sound different depending on what you touch it to. The structure of the solid matter determines the quality of the sound you hear. The pitch remains middle C, but the quality changes.

Resonance also results from air molecules being set into motion. Musical wind instruments work on the principle of air chamber resonance. Middle C played on a flute sounds different from the same note played on a tuba because of the resonating qualities of their structures. The same is true of a cello and a violin. The fundamental frequency played may be the same, but the quality we hear is very different.

Anatomy of Vocal Resonance

Our voices work on the same principle as a wind instrument. Sound begins with the vocal folds setting air into motion. These sound waves created at the vocal folds are then resonated in the cavities of the throat, mouth, and nose. The fundamental pitch established at the vocal folds is important, but equally important is the manner in which this pitch is resonated.

Variables of Vocal Resonance

Sound waves react in specific ways depending on the cavities they encounter. The harmonics, or secondary vibrations (overtones), created along with the fundamental pitch are either enriched or damped off (killed) depending on the type of environment they enter. All resonating bodies have a natural frequency at which they resonate best. Consequently, they will damp some harmonics and emphasize the amplitude of those closest to the natural frequency of the resonating body.

A jug band is a good example of this. If you blow over a big jug you hear a deep sound. A small jug produces a high, shrill sound. You may blow over these with the same intensity, but as the air rushes around inside the jug some sound waves are damped and others are emphasized. A larger cavity allows more low-pitched or long sound waves to survive. Smaller cavities damp the long sound waves, and a higher pitch results.

There are four principles of tube or cavity resonance that specifically affect speech. Vocal resonance is affected by:

1) the length of the tube or size of the cavity it passes through (larger cavities resonate lower frequencies),
2) the elasticity of the walls of the tube or cavity (softer, more relaxed surfaces resonate lower frequencies),
3) the size of the lip opening of the tube or cavity (smaller openings resonate lower frequencies),
4) the constriction along the tube or cavity.

These principles apply to the jug band, our speech, and any sound-producing source. Just like the jug band, we can alter the size of our resonating cavities to make our voices sound richer or thinner. We have three basic resonating cavities that affect our vocal sound: the pharynx, oral cavity, and nasal cavity.

Pharynx

The pharynx is a soft-sided, muscular tube about five inches long that begins at the larynx and goes up to the nasal cavity (see Figure 6). You see the back wall of this tube in a mirror when you open your mouth and say "ah." If you think of human resonating cavities as being in an "F" shape, the main, upright line would be the pharynx.

```
P NOSE
H
A MOUTH
R
Y
N
X
```

The pharynx is important for vocal resonance because it gives tube resonance to our voices. Just like the body of a clarinet or any wind instrument, the tube of the pharynx provides air trapped in a cylinder that will vibrate. Like any resonating body, a tube has a natural frequency at which it resonates best. A pipe organ or a xylophone is designed with this in mind. The resonating tubes vary in length corresponding to the notes they are to resonate. The longer tubes resonate the lower frequencies.

Our vocal resonance is affected by the length of our pharynx. A child's pharynx, for example, is short, which works best for higher frequency resonance. Because a child's vocal folds are also short and produce a high-pitched sound, the pharynx is appropriate to resonate a child's voice.

Adult voices sound more resonant if the pharynx is longer and has a greater diameter. For the most part, this is an anatomical feature and not something that can be controlled during speech.

Figure 6
Resonating Cavities

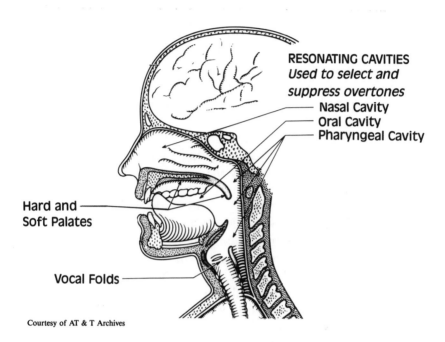

RESONATING CAVITIES
Used to select and suppress overtones
Nasal Cavity
Oral Cavity
Pharyngeal Cavity

Hard and
Soft Palates

Vocal Folds

Courtesy of AT & T Archives

One adjustment in the pharynx that does take place involves the larynx rising for a higher pitched sound and lowering for low-pitched sounds (see Focus on Phonation in Chapter 2). This may be an attempt to match the length of the pharynx with the pitch of the sound. This happens automatically just as the larynx rises and the pharynx constricts when you swallow. I have seen broadcasters, however, who purposefully constrict their necks by lowering their chins and pushing their heads back. This action seems to lower the pitch, but it increases tension in the throat area and also shortens the pharynx.

The elasticity of the walls of the pharynx also affects the quality of the resonance. A relaxed throat creates the best atmosphere for good resonance. A hard, tense throat may emphasize the higher harmonics of the voice, resulting in a harsh, strident voice. A relaxed throat usually results in a longer, softer pharynx, which produces a mellow, rich voice.

Oral Cavity

Our mouths are our most flexible resonators. We can vary the shape by moving the tongue, jaw, cheeks, and velum (soft palate). The oral cavity is also changed by any addition to the mouth, like dental braces, bridge work, or false teeth. Even tooth bonding slightly changes the resonance characteristics of the oral cavity. The tonsils lie directly behind the oral cavity in the pharangeal area, and their removal greatly changes the shape of the resonating cavities.

The tongue is a major factor in oral resonance. It fills the bottom of the mouth and continues down to form the front of the pharynx. Manipulating the tongue helps us articulate our sounds and resonate them. For the "ee" sound, for example, we raise and tense the tongue to fill part of our oral cavity. Compare the formation of the "ee" sound to "ah."

The vowels in our language are produced mainly by adjusting the shape of our oral cavity. We change its size to accentuate certain harmonics and reduce others. The same pitch, therefore, can sound like an "ee" or an "ah" based on our manipulation of the oral cavity that changes the resonance (see Focus on Resonance).

Anyone who can talk like Donald Duck knows that this is accomplished by bunching the tongue in the back of the mouth to limit the size of the resonating cavity. Likewise, Truman Capote's distinctive voice resulted from small resonating cavities. Pee Wee Herman produces a similar voice by changing his resonance. Experiment with this feeling by saying your name first with the tongue down and then with it pushed high up in the mouth toward the hard palate. By making the oral cavity smaller, you reduce the size of the resonating cavity. Just like the sound coming from the small jug, the voice sounds higher pitched.

Unfortunately, many speakers have developed a habit of bunching the tongue up in the mouth while speaking. This produces the thin, immature-sounding voice that plagues some female (and occasionally male) broadcasters, and contributes to the nasality or palatal production of certain sounds in the midwestern and New York dialects. For both these problems, opening the mouth more and lowering the tongue is the key to improvement (see Resonance Warm-Ups).

The jaw also plays an important role in oral resonance. Good flexibility of the jaw helps create a better opening. It is not surprising that the jaw often causes difficulties with resonance. The closing muscles of the jaw are some of the strongest in our body because they are designed for chewing. We often hold tension in the jaw area and clench our mouths shut. Many people do this while sleeping, and they may even grind their teeth at night. If you tend to hold your mouth tightly closed and clench your teeth at night, it is difficult to relax the jaw for speaking. You should concentrate on exercises to relax the jaw (see Resonance and Articulation Warm-Ups in this chapter and Chapter 4).

For good oral resonance, the jaw should be relaxed and free-moving. Eliminating tension from the neck area before speaking is important (see Appendix D and Phonation and Resonance Warm-Ups in this chapter and Chapter 2). Proper abdominal-diaphragmatic breathing assists in maintaining a relaxed throat (see Breathing Warm-Ups in Chapter 1). It is also a good idea to consciously try to keep space between your teeth during the day. Resist clenching your teeth. This will help your voice sound better and reduce tension in your vocal mechanism.

It is not advisable to smile when speaking. When you smile, you pull the cheek muscles back and tense them. You also have a wider mouth opening. One of the characteristics of resonance is that the smaller the mouth opening, the lower the frequencies resonated. Spreading the lips in a smile increases the size of the mouth opening and can contribute to the production of a high-pitched, strident sound. It is not accidental that most beauty pageant contestants sound alike. Their perpetual smiles have a negative affect on their resonating cavities.

You should make the most of your mouth as a resonating cavity since it is the most flexible resonator. It is amazing what can be accomplished when the mouth is improved as a resonating cavity. When clients come to me saying they want to lower their pitch, what they are usually seeking is more resonance. Remember, the flute and the tuba can play exactly the same pitch, but it sounds completely different. This difference is created by changing the resonance of the sound after it leaves the mouthpiece of the musical instrument. All of us can change our vocal sound as well by resonating it differently.

Nasal Cavity

The nasal cavity is another resonating area that can change our sound significantly. We all have heard the whining, honking sound of someone with a nasal voice. This type of voice is unpleasant because the nasal cavity is not as good at resonating as the oral cavity.

Our nasal cavities are the least controllable of the resonating areas. The nasal cavity is about four inches long and is divided by the septum, which is a wall of cartilage and bone running from our nostrils to the soft palate. The septum extends upward from the roof of the hard palate to the bottom of the brain cavity.

The septum and the mucous in the nasal cavity tend to damp low-frequency sound waves. A sound that would be full and resonate coming out of our mouths becomes high and whiny coming from our noses. The frequency of the sound may be the same when it enters the cavities, but the size of the available resonating area in each damps and reinforces different harmonics, thus changing the sound.

The soft palate (velum) works as a trap door at the back of the oral cavity (see Figure 6). It opens and closes to allow access to the nasal cavity. During respiration, the soft palate is relaxed in a downward position, which allows air to enter the pharynx from the nose. When we speak, however, the soft palate tenses and moves up and back to close off the nasal cavity (except for the three American nasal consonant sounds, /m/, /n/, and /ŋ/ (as in sing)).

To feel the soft palate working, breathe in through your nose and out through your mouth. To watch this process, hold a mirror in front of your face and open your mouth wide as you breathe. You may see the uvula, the bulb-like extension of the soft palate, pulling up into the velum as it rises. The uvula adds little to our speech or to the action of the velum, but it does help demonstrate the action of the soft palate.

The soft palate is relatively slow-moving for a speech organ. Because it must close the nasal cavity to prevent nasality on inappropriate sounds, its slow action can create difficulties.

Common Resonance Problems

Nasality

With the exception of thin voices, nasality is the most common resonance problem I hear from broadcasters. The problem occurs in various ways. Some clients have **generalized nasality,** which means all their sounds go through the nasal cavity, and a true nasal voice results. Others have **assimilated nasality,** which occurs only on vowels that precede or follow /m/, /n/, or /ŋ/. This is caused by the slow-moving nature of the soft palate. In a word like "man," for example, the soft palate remains down for the vowel sound instead of rising to close off the nose for the vowel, and then relaxing again for the /n/. Still other clients have nasality or palatal placement of certain vowels, like the midwestern and New York tendency to become nasal on the vowel sounds /ɑ/ (as in "park") and /æ/ (as in "back").

There are some anatomical reasons for nasality. A cleft palate leaves a hole in the hard palate, which allows sounds to enter the nasal cavity. This is generally corrected at birth now, but in the past, cleft palate sufferers had generalized nasality all their lives. Another problem occurs when the soft palate is too short. Also, some neurological diseases, like myasthenia gravis, affect the use of muscles and, therefore, weaken the muscles of the soft palate, limiting its ability to contract and rise to close off the nasal cavity.

In most cases, however, nasality is either a learned behavior or the result of a lazy soft palate. Learned nasality may come from living in an area where nasality pervades pronunciation patterns, or copying a parent or teacher with this sound. The soft palate may lack the needed tension to close the nasal cavity. It may also result from the mouth not being opened widely enough, which can force sound into the nasal cavity.

Unfortunately, nasality is one of the hardest resonance problems to correct. Opening the mouth more will usually help. It is also beneficial to work on placement (see Resonance Warm-Ups). I have had clients who profited from lowering their pitch, but this should only be attempted with the help of a trained speech professional.

Denasality

Many people mistakenly refer to a denasal voice as nasal. Actually, denasality is the reverse of nasality. A denasal voice sounds less nasal and is often associated with a head cold. A person might say, "I have a cold id by dose," when they are speaking with a denasal voice. For this vocal production, the nasal consonants /m/, /n/, and /ŋ/ are prevented from entering the nasal cavity. This eliminates the degree of nasality that is expected in American speech.

Denasality is usually a structural problem that requires medical attention. It results from nasopharyngeal blockage that prevents sound from entering the nose. This might be a deviated septum or a growth in the nasal cavity. Allergies can also cause blockage in the nose due to swelling and secretions. And, of course, all of us occasionally suffer from head colds that change our voices. Colds will go away, but any of the other conditions should be checked by an ear, nose, and throat specialist. Removing the blockage and perhaps follow-up speech therapy will generally eliminate the denasality.

If denasality is not caused from blockage, it may be a learned behavior. Exercises to feel the soft palate movement will aid in correcting the problem (see Focus on Resonance).

Thin Voice

The most common resonance problem I encounter in broadcasters is a thin voice. This is also referred to as an immature or
childish voice. Truman Capote's voice and parts of Pee Wee
Herman's delivery offer examples of thin voices taken to ex-
tremes. In broadcasters, a thin voice lacks an authoritative
sound. It is difficult to sound credible when you have a
child-like voice. In addition, when the volume is raised, this
voice usually becomes shrill and strident.

Bunching the tongue up in the mouth reduces the size
of the resonating cavity. When the size of a cavity is reduced, the
long sound waves are more likely to be damped. If you fill a vase
with water, you will hear this phenomenon. The pitch of the
sound coming from the water will get higher and higher as the
water fills more and more of the resonating air chamber. Most
of us know when to turn off the water by the sound we hear
from the vase.

If you use your tongue to restrict the size of your oral
cavity, you will limit the number of long sound waves that can
escape from your mouth. Your pitch will sound higher, and your
voice will sound thin. You may be speaking in your optimum
pitch range, but your small oral resonating cavity is killing the
lower-pitched harmonics and emphasizing the ones closest to its
natural resonant frequency. Because the cavity is small, its
natural resonating frequency is high. What we hear is a thin,
high-pitched sound.

Building a rich voice requires opening your mouth
more. This does not mean you will have exaggerated lip movements for speech. Your lips may not have to open any more than
they already do. What needs to be accomplished for good oral
resonance is a wider opening in the back of the oral cavity.
Arthur Lessac refers to this as the "inverted megaphone"
approach (see Suggested Reading). If you put a small megaphone next to your cheeks, the small end would be at your lips
and the wide end by your molars.

Learning to open the mouth wider in the back requires
practice. Remember that the muscles that close the mouth are
some of the strongest in our bodies. Dropping and relaxing the

jaw means letting go of tension in the jaw area (see Warm-Ups and Focus on Resonance). A reduction of tension in this area can be accomplished, however, and the increase in resonance can be dramatic.

If you are told your pitch is too high for broadcasting, the first thing you should pursue is work on resonance. You may be using your optimum pitch, but you are sending it out through a flute instead of a tuba. Spend time doing the Resonance Warm-Ups before considering artificially lowering your pitch, which can result in problems with your vocal mechanism (and remember, pitch work should always be done with the help of a trained speech professional). You may find, as many of my clients have, that increasing your resonance gives you the sound you desire. Lowering the tongue, eliminating tension in the oral cavity, and opening the mouth and throat more are all necessary steps toward better resonance.

Placement

Another aspect of resonance is placement. Placement involves where you channel the sound waves as they come up the pharynx. If the sound waves are sent straight up the pharynx, they are likely to go into the nasal or palatal area (see Figure 6). Since these areas limit good resonance, they should not be your area of placement.

To send your sound waves into the best location for good oral resonance, you should place the sound just behind your upper front teeth. This requires bringing the sound waves up the pharynx and making a ninety degree turn into the oral cavity. It also involves sensing the vibrations extending all the way to the front teeth. Breath is a key here, since it is the energy for speech. Be certain that you are using proper breathing as described in Chapter 1.

I ask clients to visualize their placement in some manner. Some view the sound waves as a garden hose coming up from their lungs and spraying out their mouths. Others see a beam of colored light projecting from their lungs, turning to enter the oral cavity, and extending forward to their front teeth and out their mouth. I even had one radio sports announcer who envisioned his placement as a basketball being thrown in an arch.

An especially good image was suggested by voice coach Betty May Collins Parker. She suggests to her clients that they imagine the curved area of the mouth above the alveolar ridge (ridge behind the upper front teeth) to be a cup. She asks them to pour sound into the cup and fill the cup with sound as they speak until they can feel vibrations in the cup area.

Whatever image works for you is fine as long as it helps you sense where the sound waves should be channeled into the oral cavity for the most effective resonance.

Good resonance should be the goal of all broadcasters. Letting our natural resonators, the pharynx, nose, and mouth, do their optimum work produces the best voice with the least amount of strain.

Focus on Resonance

To improve the resonance of your voice, you must first learn to feel the involvement of your resonators in your speech production.

A) Use a mirror to watch the movement of the soft palate. Inhale through your nose and exhale through your mouth. Watch the uvula (the bulb-like extension of the soft palate) move up and down. It moves up when the soft palate rises, closing like a trap door to block the nasal cavity as you exhale out of your mouth. When you inhale, the back of the tongue moves up to meet the soft palate as it relaxes in its downward position.

B) Now watch the movement of your soft palate and tongue as you make the following sounds:

- gah, gah, gah, gah
- ng, ng, ng, ng (as in "sing")
- ah, ah, ah, ah (as in "father")
- ah, ng, ah, ng

C) The tightest closure of the soft palate occurs for the consonant plosive sounds of /p/ /b/ and /t/ /d/. These sounds are called plosives because the air must be stopped in our mouths and pressure must build up before the air is allowed to explode out. Feel the soft palate's tight closure by making these sounds. Exaggerate the build-up of air before letting it explode out. Now begin the formation of the /p/ sound and build up extra pressure. Instead of letting it explode, release the pressure through your nose. You should feel the soft palate relaxing to let the air out the nose. You may even feel some popping in your ears.

D) To check for denasality, breathe through each nostril alone when your nasal cavity is clear. If one nostril restricts your air intake, you will feel it. Watch in a mirror as you do this. One nostril may seem to collapse when you inhale through it. You may see this at the nostril or higher up behind the bridge of the nose. Closure is a sign that there is some blockage in that nostril. You might want to have this checked by a physician. To hear the effect of denasality, hold your nostrils closed and say this phrase:

> Now our morning money market
> summary.

With denasality, it probably sounded like

> Dow our bordig bodey barket subary.

This illustrates the important role our nasal consonants play in giving our language its distinctive sound.

E) To check for nasality, hold your nose closed and repeat the following sentences:

> Authorities agree that the gas
> could have caused the fire.
>
> The reporter will follow the story
> at six o'clock.

These sentences have no nasal sounds in them. When you hold your nose closed and say them, you should not feel any pressure in the nasal area. If you do, you have nasality to some degree. The pressure comes because you are allowing some sound to enter the nasal cavity. You feel it trying to escape from your closed nose.

F) To feel nasal resonance at work, try making the three nasal sounds. Make a strong /m/ sound by closing your lips and forcing the air into the nasal cavity. Put your index finger and thumb on the bridge of your nose and feel the vibrations as you make the sound. Now make an /n/ sound by putting the tip of your tongue against the alveolar ridge (the ridge behind the upper front teeth) and blocking the air. Again, feel the vibrations. Now make an /ŋ/ sound as in "sing." Bring your tongue up to your velum, and feel the vibrations. Next alternate between "ah" and /m/, and feel the change in vibrations. You should feel the nose vibrating for the /m/, but no vibrations with "ah."

G) To get a sense of your pharynx moving, induce a comfortable, relaxed yawn. This opens the pharynx for the maximum intake of air. Use this as a natural relaxer for the throat.

H) To illustrate how smiling affects your voice, say the vowel "ah" with the lips pulled back. Now say the vowel without a smile by dropping the jaw straight down. Listen to the difference in the quality of the sound. The first one should sound thinner and more tense than the second. You may think the pitch is different, but you should try to keep it the same. The change in the quality of the sound can be quite apparent, and it can result from the change in resonance only.

I) Our vowels are formed by changing the shape of our oral cavity, which alters the resonance. Say these vowels, gliding from one to another, and feel the oral cavity adjusting for each vowel:

- "ah"—"ee"—"awe"—"oo" (as in food).

Resonance Warm-Ups

When doing the resonance Warm-Ups, especially the ones that call for opening the back of the mouth more, you should use some caution. Do not force the jaw open too widely. This is of utmost importance if you have TMJ syndrome (temporomandibular joint dysfunction) or have had dislocations of your jaw. Symptoms of these would be pain when chewing or talking, tightness in the jaw, and clicking sounds with jaw movement. If you have any of these symptoms, open only as wide as you can without straining when you do these Warm-Ups, and consult a dental specialist to relieve the jaw problem.

1) To improve placement and increase oral resonance, bend forward from the waist at a ninety degree angle. Keep your neck straight so you are looking down at the floor. Flex your knees slightly to prevent strain on your back. (If you have a bad back, do this Warm-Up on all fours with your back straight and your face parallel to the floor.) Repeat this phrase, aiming the sound at the floor as you look down:

- Good evening, this is (your name)
  reporting for Eyewitness News.

Feel the sound resonating in your oral cavity before the sound falls toward the floor. Concentrate on hitting the floor with the sound. Now straighten up and repeat the phrase, keeping the placement the same.

2) The sound "ah" opens the mouth the widest and lowers the tongue. Doctors use this to look at our throats, and you can use it to increase resonance. Say the following words, preceded by "ah," and try to maintain the wide opening:

ah	far
ah	father
ah	got
ah	factor
ah	back

ah	tackle
ah	awesome
ah	awful
ah	law
ah	go
ah	own
ah	gold

3) The word "awe" puts your lips and cheeks in a position to have the best oral resonance. This position is the reverse of a smile, which pulls the lips back and tenses the cheeks. Say the word "awe" before each number as you count from one to ten to feel the relaxed, forward position of the cheeks and lips.

- Awe—1, awe—2, awe—3, etc.

4) To increase the opening in the back of the mouth, make a fist with your hand and extend the index and middle finger slightly. With these fingers still in a bent position, place the knuckles against your cheek with your thumb toward the ground. The desired effect is to use the knuckles of your two bent fingers to measure an opening of an inch or more between your molars. Press these fingers against your cheek and open your mouth enough to push your knuckles between your molars. This creates a wide opening in the back of the mouth. With your fingers in this position, say these words (they may sound distorted):

- go, go, go, go
- awe, awe, awe, awe
- ah, ah, ah, ah
- at, at, at, at
- all, all, all, all
- yard, yard, yard, yard

Use the knuckles of your index and middle fingers to measure an opening between your molars.

Courtesy of WVIR–TV, Charlottesville, VA

5) Preserving the feeling of the last Warm-Up, leave your bent fingers against your cheeks. This time let them be a gauge of the size of the opening sustained while speaking. You will feel your teeth come together for some sounds, but try to maintain the wide opening when possible. Repeat these sentences, working to open the back of the mouth:

```
Good afternoon. This is Newsbreak,
and I'm (your name).

    Fighting broke out again today
between rival forces.

    Winter promises to bring bitter
cold to the Washington area.

    A victory today for abortion
rights supporters.
```

6) To increase jaw openness for better resonance, place your chin between your thumb and index finger. Repeat these words, feeling the jaw drop as much as possible:

- back, back, back, back
- sack, sack, sack, sack
- bad, bad, bad, bad
- yard, yard, yard, yard
- am, am, am, am
- accent, accent, accent, accent
- sang, sang, sang, sang

7) To avoid assimilated nasality, you must learn to keep vowels that precede or follow nasal sounds from having nasal production. This requires extra work to close the nasal cavity for these vowel sounds. Practice with these comparisons. The first column should be resonated in the oral cavity. Check your production of this by holding your nose closed while you say a word in the first column. You should be able to say all the words in the first column with no air pressure against your closed nose. Next say the corresponding word in the second column, but maintain the oral resonance for the first part of the word. You can hold your nose closed until you get to the nasal sound at the end of the word to monitor your oral placement.

be	beam
tee	team
see	seam
we	wing
law	long
pay	pain
owe	own
burr	burn

In the next two columns, say the nasal sound in the first column, but in the second column, switch to oral resonance for the rest of the word after the nasal.

m	me
m	mud
m	mow
m	mitt
n	no
n	near
n	new
n	need

8) It is important to continue to work on placement of the sound waves behind the front teeth. Decide what imagery you want to use to see the sound beginning at the diaphragm and moving up from the lungs through the vocal folds and into the pharynx. Watch the sound waves making the important ninety degree turn to enter the oral cavity, and see the sound waves hitting the back of the front teeth or the cup above the alveolar ridge before leaving the mouth. You might think of a beam of light, a hose, a tube, or anything that helps you visualize this path. Now repeat these vowel sounds with your eyes closed and your concentration on the sound waves making their journey:

- ah, awe, eee

- ah, awe, eee

- ah, awe, eee

Next say this sentence with the same concentration:

- My voice begins at the diaphragm, is pushed from the lungs, passes through the vocal folds into the pharynx, and turns to resonate in my oral cavity.

Keep working with this phrase until you can say it with one exhalation and imagine it moving through the vocal mechanism.

Being conversational does not mean being sloppy or regionalistic. It takes constant work and study to make the audience listen to what is said, not who is saying it. The job of a communicator is to make it sound easy to do, even though it isn't.

Bob Bartlett
News Director, KTAB–TV
Abilene, Texas

The regional or ethnic accent may be the most important to attack. Viewers and listeners will question the credibility of someone who obviously doesn't sound like they are from "around here."

Al Nash
News Director, KTVQ
Billings, Montana

Articulation— Forming and Shaping the Sound

A healthy, well-resonated sound is worthless to you as a broadcaster and a communicator if you cannot articulate the sound into words. Words in our language are made up of phonemes (individual sounds) that combine to give meaning. We use our articulators to shape sound waves into phonemes.

Proper articulation is of utmost importance to you as a broadcaster because your voice must be carried through many different electronic devices (see Figure 7). You speak into a microphone which transfers the sound to an amplifier which is connected to a transmitter. After the sound is transmitted either by wires or satellite, it must go through a receiver and be broadcast through a speaker before it can enter the listener's ear. Every step in this process can diminish the sound. What might be heard perfectly well in face-to-face conversation may be washed out by the time it reaches the listener in electronic media. Careful articulation is imperative.

Articulation Anatomy

To shape sound, we use our lips, teeth, tongue, jaw, and hard and soft palate (see Figure 8). These structures are called our articulators. We move our articulators in many ways to speak, and they are most active for consonants.

To feel the articulation of a series of consonants, first make a /p/ sound. The lips come together to stop the air and let it explode out to make the /p/. Now try a "th" sound. Begin to say the word "thin" and feel the friction that results from forcing air through the opening between the front teeth and the tongue. Now make a /t/ sound and feel the tongue tip coming in contact with the alveolar ridge. The soft palate helps with the production of /k/ and /g/ sounds. The tongue comes up to contact the soft palate. Begin to say the word "kick" and feel this movement.

Vowel sounds are made by changing the shape of the oral cavity, thereby changing the resonance. Compare the "ee" sound with "ah." The "ee" sound is produced with a limited mouth opening and a tense, high tongue. For "ah" the jaw and

Figure 7
Electronic Communication

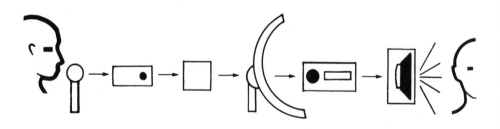

Microphone Amplifier Transmitter Satellite Receiver   Speaker

Figure 8
Articulators

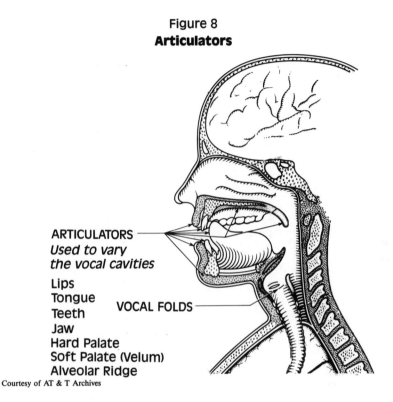

ARTICULATORS
*Used to vary
the vocal cavities*

Lips
Tongue   VOCAL FOLDS
Teeth
Jaw
Hard Palate
Soft Palate (Velum)
Alveolar Ridge
Courtesy of AT & T Archives

tongue drop to increase the size of the resonating cavity. All vowels depend on the tension of the mouth, the height of the tongue, and the shape of the lips for their production.

Flexibility

The expressions "lazy tongue" or "lazy mouth" indicate the importance of flexibility for good articulation. If the articulators are sluggish, it is difficult to articulate sounds clearly. Frequently this is referred to as "sloppy speech." Sometimes this is adequate in relaxed conversation, but poor articulation is never acceptable for broadcast voice.

The agility of our articulators is very important for good speech. Consider, for example, what your tongue alone has to do to say a simple sentence like, "Let Ted label that truck." Say the sentence slowly and feel the tongue moving from the alveolar ridge to the front teeth and up to the soft palate (see Figure 8). The tongue must make all this movement to produce only five words. At this rate, the tongue will make as many as 300 or more movements a minute to produce speech.

Tongue positions are only one part of the complicated combination of articulation movements required for speech. While the tongue is moving, the jaw must vary the size of the oral cavity and the soft palate must open and close the passage to the nasal cavity. All of this must be done rapidly to create the series of phonemes that make up speech. Watching an X-ray of the speech process is like seeing a finely tuned machine in motion, making hundreds of adjustments every minute.

The jaw is of utmost importance in the process of articulation. Even the most flexible tongue cannot move freely if the jaw is constricting the oral cavity. Clenched teeth not only affect resonance (see Chapter 3), but they limit the movement of the other articulators as well. Developing an open, relaxed mouth is important for both resonance and articulation (see Resonance and Articulation Warm-ups in this chapter and Chapter 3).

The articulators depend on lubrication to work properly, just like the vocal folds. Unlike the rest of the vocal tract, however, which produces mucous for lubrication, the oral cavity produces saliva. Glands under the tongue and in the back of the mouth secrete saliva. Dehydration causes a reduction in saliva, which makes articulation more difficult (see Chapter 2). Tension also may reduce the production of saliva. Public speakers are provided with a glass of water for this reason. Taking a few sips of water lubricates the mouth and relaxes the throat. You can also activate the salivary glands by sucking as if you had a mint in your mouth. You will feel the saliva coming out from under the tongue as you pretend you are sucking a mint.

Tension can also cause too much saliva to be produced. A radio client of mine called one day to ask my advice about excessive saliva. She said she had to swallow throughout her newscast because her mouth was flooded with saliva. I imagined her using a towel to wipe her mouth as the saliva poured out, but she assured me it was not quite that severe. She was worried, however, that her new job would be in jeopardy because of the problem. Using breathing exercises to relax, she overcame her tension about her new job. When the tension disappeared, so did the excess saliva.

The Sounds of Our Language

In order to articulate properly, you must know the sounds we use in our language and how to form them correctly. There are forty sounds (phonemes) required for General American speech. General American is the dialect most accepted for broadcasters.

Because we have an alphabet that uses twenty-six letters to represent forty sounds, our spelling is confusing. We cannot depend on written words for pronunciation guides. In order to know how to pronounce words, we have to depend on a more accurate system than our alphabet and spelling. We must use a sound-based method as a guide to pronunciation.

A **phoneme** is the smallest segment of sound we can produce that signals meaning. (Phonemes are printed in slash marks to distinguish the symbol for the sound from a letter in our alphabet.) If you omit the /t/ sound from the word "last," for example, you have the word "lass." Therefore, /t/ is a phoneme in the word "last." "Last" contains four phonemes: /l/, the vowel sound /æ/, /s/, and /t/. "Lass" has only three phonemes: /l/, /æ/, and /s/. Likewise, if you omit the /r/ from "crash," you have the word "cash." Phonemes signal meaning in our words.

Phonemes and spelling are not always the same, which makes our language difficult to learn to pronounce. Look at the word "thaw." It is spelled with four letters, but there are only two phonemes in the word: the /θ/ ("th" sound) and the vowel sound "aw" /ɔ/. "Bought" has six letters and only three sounds: /b/, the vowel /ɔ/, and /t/. We also have the spelling problem of silent letters like the extra "s" in the word "lass" /læs/.

Another problem with our spelling that creates pronunciation difficulty is that many of our sounds are spelled with the same letter. The letter, "e," for example, can be pronounced in six different ways: /ɑ/ as in "sergeant," /e/ as in "Jose," /i/ as in "be," /ɪ/ as in "pretty," /ɛ/ as in "pen," and /ə/ as in "item." Consider the different pronunciations of the vowel sounds represented by "ou" in the following words: through, though, thought, rough, could, loud.

There is also the problem of the same sound having different spellings. For example, the /i/ ("ee" sound) can be spelled in at least ten different ways, including "Caesar," "see," "eve" and "please." A frequently used example of this is said to have been given by George Bernard Shaw. He wrote the word "ghoti," and asked for it to be pronounced. When he reported it was the word "fish" he explained that the "gh" was as in "rough," the "o" was as in "women," and the "ti" was as in "nation."

Finding Proper Pronunciations

Knowing the proper pronunciations of words is a requirement for a good broadcaster. The *United Press International Broadcast Stylebook* says that it is as important for a broadcaster to know how to pronounce words correctly as it is for a newspaper writer to know how to spell them. As broadcasters, you have an obligation to the public to set a standard for correct pronunciation.

In the past, networks have often provided help with establishing standard pronunciations. Dr. Cabell Greet, a former professor at Barnard College, was a pronunciation and grammar consultant for CBS for nearly fifteen years. He carefully screened broadcasts and sent memos to reporters when corrections were needed. Today, broadcasters usually are responsible for polishing their own pronunciations.

There are three places you can look when you need to find the proper pronunciation of a word:

1. the dictionary,

2. the wire service,

3. a phonetic dictionary.

The Dictionary

You are probably familiar with the use of a dictionary for pronunciation. Dictionaries use a system called diacritical markings to show pronunciations of each word they list. These markings can be helpful, but they are sometimes hard to decipher because they vary from publisher to publisher. Also, they depend on unfamiliar markings like macrons (a line above a letter), umlauts (two dots above a letter), and breves (a curved line above a letter).

If you are marking your script to help you remember the pronunciation of a particular word, diacritical markings do not always work well. The markings above letters can be difficult to see, and the system may be hard to remember.

The Wire Service

The wire services offer daily pronunciation guides for difficult words and names (see Figure 9). Phonetic spellings or "pronouncers" are given, using the letters of our alphabet. Here is the key to the UPI broadcast pronunciation style, taken from the *United Press International Broadcast Stylebook:*

A

AY for long A (as in mate)
A for short A (as in cat)
AI for nasal A (as in air)
AH for soft A (as in father)
AW for broad A (as in talk)

E

EE for long E (as in meat)
EH for short E (as in get)
UH for hollow E (as in the, or French prefix le)
AY for French long E with acute accent (as in Pathe)

IH for middle E (as in pretty)
EW for EW diphthong (as in few)

I

IGH for long I (as in time)
EE for French long I (as in machine)
IH for short I (as in pity)

O

OH for long O (as in note, or "ough" as in though)
AH for short O (as in hot)
AW for broad O (as in fought)
OO for long double OO (as in fool, or "ough" as in through)
UH for short double O (as in foot, or "ouch" as in touch)
OW for OW diphthong (as in how, or "ough" as in plough)

U

EW for long U (as in mule)
OO for long U (as in rule)
U for middle U (as in put)
UH for short U (as in shut)

Consonants

K for hard C (as in cat)
S for soft C (as in cease)
SH for soft CH (as in machine)
CH for hard CH or TCH (as in catch)
Z for hard S (as in disease)
S for soft S (as in sun)
G for hard G (as in gang)

J for soft G (as in general)
ZH for soft J (as in French version of Joliet)

This system is helpful, but it is limited because it is based on the letters of our alphabet. It is impossible to give a phonetic transcription of every word in our language using only

Figure 9
UPI Daily Pronunciation Guide

```
z0224
d v bc-World-Prono-Guide 0463
  -11-(
  AOUN, Michel (MEE'-shehl Aw-OON'), general, Lebanese military
leader(
    Apartheid (uh-PAHR'-tayt), South African racial separation policy(
    BOESAK (Boo-sak), Allan, anti-apartheid South African clergyman(
    Bogota (BOH'-goh-TAH'), Colombia(
    BOTHA, Roelof ''Pik'' (ROO'-lawf Pihk BOH'-tah), South African
foreign minister(
    Cartagena (Kahr-tuh-HAYN'-yuh), city in Colombia(
    GENSCHER, Hans-Dietrich (DEE'-trihk GEHN'-shehr), West German
foreign minister(
    GERASIMOV, Gennadi (Gehn-NAH'-dee Gehr-AH'-see-mawf), Soviet
Foreign Ministry spokesman(
    GORBACHEV, Mikhail (MEEK'-high-yehl GOHRB'-ah-chawf), Soviet
president(
    GYSI, Gregor (GREH'-gohr GEE'-see), East German Communist Party
chief(
    Halle (HAH'-luh), East German town(
    Hezbollah (Hehz-BOH'-lah), Islamic party in Lebanon (''Party of
God'')(
    ILIESCU, Ion (Yahn Eel-ee-EHS'-koo), interim Romanian president(
    Jihad (Zhee-HAHD'), Islamic, a pro-Khomeini terrorist group(
    KHAMENEI, Sayed Ali (Sigh-eed Ah-lee Kah-may-nee), Iranian
spiritual leader(
    KHOMEINI, AYATOLLAH RUHOLLAH (Ah-yah-toh-LAH' Roo-hoh-LAH'
Khoh-may-nee), late Iranian religious leader(
    LILOV (LEE'-lawf), Alexander, Bulgarian Communist Party chief(
    LUKANOV, Andrei (AHN'-dray Loo-KAH'-nawf), Bulgarian prime minister(
    MANDELA (Man-DEH'-lah) Nelson, freed black nationalist leader in
South Africa(
    Medellin (Meh-duh-YEEN') cartel, illegal drug organization named
after Colombian city(
    MLADENOV (Mlah-DEH'-nawf), Peter, Bulgarian foreign minister who
replaced Todor Zhivkov as president and Communist Party chief(
    MODROW, Hans (Hahns MOHD'-roh), East German prime minister(
    RUSHDIE, Salman (SAHL'-muhn RUHSH'-dee), author condemned to death
by Ayatollah Khomeini for his book ''The Satanic Verses''(
    SHEVARDNADZE (Shyeh-vahr-nahd-sheh), Eduard, Soviet foreign
minister(
    SISULU (Sih-SOO'-loo), Walter, South African black leader released
after 25 years in prison(
    Sofia (SOH'-fee-uh), Bulgaria(
    Soweto (Soh-WEH'-toh), South African black township near
Johannesburg(
    TUTU (TOO'-too), Desmond, South African Anglican archbishop, Nobel
Peace Prize Winner(
    WOERNER, Manfred (MAHN'-frehd VEHR'-nehr), NATO Secretary General(
    ZHIVKOV, Todor (TOH'-dohr ZHIHV'-kawf), resigned Bulgarian
president and Communist Party chief(
```

the alphabet. The wire services often resort to rhyming to make their pronunciations clear. UPI, for example, compares the name "Roger Blough," to the pronunciation of "now."

The main advantage of the wire service pronunciation guides is that they deal with proper names and places that are in the current news. It is advisable to save the daily pronunciation guides given by the wire services. You might want to develop your own file or notebook of these guides. This will help you pronounce the many foreign names and places that are in the news every day.

It is also a good idea to add local pronunciations to your personal guide. When you first move to a station, ask other reporters about local pronunciations. "Cairo" in Illinois, for example, is pronounced "Kayro." In Maryland, "Grosvenor" is pronounced "Grovner," and in Missouri, "New Madrid" does not sound the same as "Madrid, Spain." The emphasis is on the first syllable in the Missouri pronunciation. Your credibility with your local audience will be ruined if you mispronounce local names.

A Phonetic Dictionary

The International Phonetic Alphabet (IPA) contains hundreds of symbols to transcribe all languages. Forty of these symbols represent the most frequently used sounds in American speech. This alphabet relies on most of the twenty-six letters of our alphabet and adds ten symbols to cover all forty sounds. (The letters C, Q, Y, and X are omitted because they are represented by the sounds /k/ or /s/, /kju/, /j/, and /ɛks/.) The IPA was developed because a group of scholars attending an international convention of language teachers in 1888 were aware of the difficulty of transcribing English without a phonetic alphabet. It has been used since that time as the most accurate guide to pronunciation.

A phonetic symbol represents only one sound and does not change its pronunciation. The symbol /i/, for example, always represents the sound "ee" as in bee. When you see a word written in phonetics that includes an /i/, you can be confident that sound is "ee." The word "bee" would be written /bi/ in phonetics. Knowing this symbol, you can easily pronounce these words written in phonetics: /ti/, /ki/, /mit/, /lin/ (tea, key, meet, lean).

The advantages of using the IPA are that it is easy to learn and remember, it is easy to write on your copy, and it is the only accepted international set of symbols used for pronunciation. You will find that most speech and linguistics books use the IPA. It is also used by many foreign-language dictionaries, such as those by Cassell. Because the IPA uses most of the letters of our alphabet, it is not difficult to remember. Words you write in phonetics in your copy are easy to see and pronounce.

As a broadcaster, it is well worth the effort to commit the symbols to memory and begin using them. Once you have mastered the symbols, you will have a tool you can use the rest of your career.

Several dictionaries use phonetics for their pronunciation guide, such as *The NBC Handbook of Pronunciation* (Harper & Row) which adapts the IPA and has been a standard reference book for broadcasters for many years. Unfortunately, the publisher reports that at the present time it is indefinitely out of stock with no new edition planned in the near future.

Kenyon and Knott's *A Pronouncing Dictionary of American English* (Merriam-Webster) is considered the bible of pronunciation by most speech and linguist professionals. It is also an excellent pronunciation reference guide for broadcasters. There is a key to the IPA in the front of this dictionary, which makes it a handy reference guide whether you know the IPA or not.

Kenyon and Knott's dictionary lists only the pronunciations of words. The pronunciations are given in all three of the accepted dialects in this country: General American, Eastern, and Southern. (A word like "fare," for example, is listed as /fɛr/ for General American, /fɛə/ without the /r/ for Eastern, and /fæə/ without the /r/ and using the vowel as in "at" for Southern.) The only shortcoming of this dictionary is that it was published in 1953. Pronunciations change fairly slowly in this country, but it is a good idea to check any confusing pronunciations in a more current dictionary (see Selected References in Chapter 6).

The IPA for Broadcasters

The IPA is divided into consonants and vowels just like our alphabet (see Figure 10). These categories are then classified by the method of production.

Figure 10
The Complete International Phonetic Alphabet for American English
(See Appendix C for more practice words.)

VOICED

Vowels

/i/	bee
/ɪ/	bit
/e/	say
/ɛ/	bet
/æ/	at
/ɑ/	spa
/ɔ/	caw
/o/	oak
/u/	two
/ʊ/	put
/ə/	above
/ɚ/	father

Diphthongs

/ju/	use
/aɪ/	eye
/aʊ/	cow
/ɔɪ/	toy

Consonants			
VOICELESS		**VOICED**	
/t/	to	/d/	do
/p/	pop	/b/	boy
/k/	key	/g/	got
/f/	fit	/v/	van
/θ/	thin	/ð/	them
/s/	say	/z/	zip
/ʃ/	she	/ʒ/	casual
/h/	hit		
/tʃ/	chip	/dʒ/	Jim
		/w/	was
		/j/	yet
		/r/	run
		/l/	love
		/m/	miss
		/n/	now
		/ŋ/	sing

Vowels

Vowels in our language are all voiced, meaning that the vocal folds vibrate for their production. Vowels are formed by changes in resonance and are classified as pure vowels or diphthongs. Pure vowels can be extended indefinitely when produced. You can say /i/ ("ee"), for example, until you run out of air. Diphthongs, on the other hand, change articulation during pronunciation. They require movement of the mouth for their production, since they are composed of two vowel sounds coming together. Say the vowel in "toy," and you will feel your mouth moving for its production.

   Our usual a-e-i-o-u symbols are inadequate when it comes to representing the sixteen vowel sounds in our language. The IPA uses these symbols for the vowel phonemes (see Appendix C for more practice words):

Pure Vowels		Diphthongs	
/i/	bee	/ju/	use
/ɪ/	bit	/aɪ/	eye
/e/	say	/aʊ/	cow
/ɛ/	bet	/ɔɪ/	toy
/æ/	at		
/ɑ/	spa		
/ɔ/	caw		
/o/	oak		
/u/	two		
/ʊ/	put		
/ə/	above		
/ɚ/	father		

Consonants

To produce consonants in English we either stop or partially stop the air as it comes from the mouth. Consonants are, therefore, classified by the method of releasing the air, the position of the articulators when they are produced, and whether they are voiced or not.

Voicing is perhaps the easiest distinguishing factor of consonants. To understand the difference in voicing, put your fingers on your larynx and begin to say the word "to." Stop after you have made the /t/ sound and repeat the /t/ several times. Next make a /d/ sound as in the word "do." You should feel vibrations in your larynx for the /d/ and none for the /t/. These particular consonants are called cognates because they are articulated in the same manner, but one sound is voiced and one is voiceless. There are eight cognate pairs in our language:

Voiceless		Voiced	
/t/	to	/d/	do
/p/	pop	/b/	boy
/k/	key	/g/	got
/f/	fit	/v/	van

/θ/	"th" thin	/ð/	them
/s/	say	/z/	zip
/ʃ/	"sh" she	/ʒ/	casual
/tʃ/	"ch" chip	/dʒ/	Jim

Using the classifying method of where the air is released and the position of the articulators, the consonants are grouped in the following manner:

-Stops or Plosives-

These sounds are formed by stopping the air and letting it explode out to produce the phoneme. For the /t/ /d/ sounds, the tongue goes to the alveolar ridge to stop the air. The /p/ /b/ are formed by the lips closing to block the air. The /k/ /g/ involve the back of the tongue coming up to the soft palate to block the air (see Figure 8).

Voiceless		Voiced	
/t/	to	/d/	do
/p/	pop	/b/	boy
/k/	key	/g/	got

-Fricatives-

Fricatives result from friction created by forcing air through a small opening between the articulators. These sounds can be extended until all air has been exhausted.

Voiceless		Voiced	
/f/	fit	/v/	van
/θ/	thin	/ð/	them
/s/	say	/z/	zip
/ʃ/	she	/ʒ/	casual
/h/	hit		

-Affricates-

These two sounds are similar to fricatives, but they include a plosive. Unlike the fricatives, their production cannot be extended because of the plosive included in each phoneme.

Voiceless	**Voiced**
/tʃ/ chip	/dʒ/ Jim

-Glides-

Glides are distinguished by the movement of the tongue during formation. They are also affected by vowel sounds and are sometimes called semivowels. The /w/ sound is the only glide that can be voiced or voiceless, but the voicing is difficult to distinguish.

Voiced

/w/   was
/j/   yet
/r/   run

-Lateral-

The /l/ sound is unique in our language. All our phonemes are produced by sending the sound straight out of the mouth or up through the nose except for the /l/ sound. This phoneme is produced by putting the tip of the tongue on the alveolar ridge (see Figure 8) and holding it there while the sides of the tongue drop. The sound is then allowed to escape from the mouth over the edges of the tongue.

Voiced

/l/   love

-Nasals-

These sounds are produced by closing off the oral cavity and allowing the sound waves to enter the nasal cavity. For the /m/ our lips come together to block the air. The /n/ sound is formed by the tongue rising to make contact with the side teeth and the alveolar ridge to block the air. For the /ŋ/ sound, the back of the tongue and the soft palate come together to block the air, forcing it to escape through the nose.

Voiced

/m/	miss
/n/	now
/ŋ/	sing

Articulation Problems

There are three basic ways in which our articulation can be faulty. We can omit necessary sounds, substitute or add sounds, or produce sounds incorrectly.

Omissions

Consonants cause the most problems involving omissions of sounds. This is unfortunate for broadcasters because consonants are so important to intelligibility and credibility. Broadcasting makes the omission problem worse because consonants often lose strength when sent through electronic media (see Figure 7).

Consonants add clarity to our language. If you say the word "oil" so that it sounds like "all," most people still know what you mean even though you are saying the vowel incorrectly. If you omit the /l/, however, you are no longer clear to your listener, even if the vowel is perfectly pronounced. Without proper consonant articulation, meaning may suffer.

One of the biggest challenges of articulation is to say your consonant phonemes correctly without sounding overpronounced. When you first begin working on pronouncing your consonants, you will most likely sound overpronounced. Only practice will eliminate the overly-precise sound.

Because consonants add clarity, it is important to form each one properly. If you say "last," for instance, and do not let the air explode out for the /t/, you have said "lass." Similarly, if you say "ass" for "ask," you have pronounced a different word. Remember that a phoneme is the smallest segment of spoken sound that signals meaning. If you leave out a phoneme, which you would be doing if you did not complete the plosive sound of the /k/ in "ask," you may be saying a different word.

The plosive consonant phonemes cause the most omission problems. The six plosive consonant phonemes are cognates:

Voiceless		Voiced	
/t/	to	/d/	do
/p/	pop	/b/	boy
/k/	key	/g/	got

These plosives require a burst of air for their production. If you hold your hand in front of your mouth, you should feel a puff of air as you say each of these phonemes.

The sentence, "Last winter the lists show it snowed two feet," requires the production of initial, medial, and final plosives. Say this sentence out loud. If it sounds like, "Lass winner the lis show i snow two fee," you know you have not pronounced your consonant plosive phonemes, and you have lost the intelligibility of the sentence.

I advise my clients to decide how precise they want their delivery to sound. Once they have decided if they want a relaxed, very conversational sound, or a more credible, precise delivery, they can begin to work on consonant plosives.

In the sentence, "Last winter the lists show it snowed two feet," everyone needs to pronounce the consonant plosives in the words "last," "two," and "feet" in order to achieve intelligibility. That would represent the least precise end of a continuum of articulation. For a more precise sound, you should also pronounce the consonant plosives in "winter" and "it." The most precise delivery would include correct pronunciation of the plosives in "lists" and "snowed." Pronouncing these last two words correctly requires very flexible articulators and practice to make the sentence sound natural.

Listening to broadcasters, you will hear omissions of consonant plosives to greater and lesser degrees. Remember the continuum as you listen to other broadcasters. Some will have very precise deliveries while others omit most plosives. Ed Bliss remembers Lowell Thomas saying he grew up hearing his father shout, "Articulate, son!" Thomas' delivery reflected this precision of articulation. You will notice that intelligibility, credibility, and precision of pronunciation are all linked. In Appendix A, you will see that 17 percent of news directors say they like a precise delivery. For this reason, working to pronounce ending and medial consonant plosives can be helpful (see Articulation Warm-Ups).

There are some problems, however, with consonant plosive production. One is that overpronouncing these endings can make you sound pedantic. This is especially true if you stress consonant plosives in nonessential words. Say, "The gunman ran, but the county police captured him." If you overpronounce the /t/ sounds in "but" and "county," you have taken away from the meaning of the sentence. You need to produce these /t/ sounds correctly, but you should not stress them.

You may find you are overpronouncing when you first begin to work on your consonant plosive production. The example sentence, "Last winter the lists show it snowed two feet," may require a great deal of practice to pronounce correctly. At first, you may sound like Eliza Doolittle in *My Fair Lady*, as you work to hit every plosive sound. The goal is for the production to be correct without drawing attention to the phonemes. This takes practice (see Articulation Warm-Ups).

Another problem associated with plosives is the popping sound that sometimes results from these phonemes. This is most noticeable on the /p/ and /b/ sounds. If you find popping is a problem, try speaking across the microphone instead of

Lowell Thomas anchored the first regularly scheduled radio network news report in 1930, and his career continued for 45 years.

Courtesy of CBS News.

directly into it. You might also find lowering the microphone away from your mouth helps. Most of the time, changing the position of the microphone will eliminate the popping. If it doesn't, talk to your engineer about the problem. Certain microphones are more sensitive to popping, and a change in microphones or a wind screen may be needed.

Substitutions

There are many possibilities for substitutions of one phoneme for another in our pronunciations. Foreign speakers, for example, often have substitution problems with five or ten different phonemes. A French speaker, for example, might say "sink" for "think." Broadcasters tend to have three substitutions that are most common.

1) /t/ and /d/ for /θ/ and /ð/

Working in the Washington, D.C., area, I have found the substitution of /t/ or /d/ for the "th" sounds to be a problem for many of my clients. This substitution has become part of a generalized speech pattern called "Big City Dialect." It does not matter if you are from D.C. or Los Angeles or New York City, this substitution is part of your dialect. One possible reason for this substitution localizing to big cities may be the fact that many foreign languages like French, German, and Spanish do not use the phonemes /θ/ and /ð/. Cities with large foreign populations suffer from the substitution because non-native speakers have difficulty forming the "th" sound. /t/ and /d/ are easier for them to use. If you live in a big city, you hear this substitution being made around you all the time, and you may begin to use it yourself.

This speech pattern is often associated with the stereotypical athlete who might say, "De coach put de tickets in dere." Few broadcasters would be this far off in the correct pronunciation of "th," but even a few substitutions can hurt your credibility. It is important to form these sounds correctly (see Articulation Warm-Ups).

2) /w/ for /l/

The /w/ /l/ substitution is also a frequent problem. This substitution affects pronunciations of words like, "bottle," "table," and "pull." Instead of producing the /l/ phoneme in these words, a /w/ is substituted. The words then sound like, "bottw," "tabw," and "puw." With this substitution, clarity is lost, and speech sounds childish.

3) /w/ for /r/

The /w/ phoneme is an easy one to produce, so it often substitutes for the /r/ sound in addition to the /l/. /r/ is a difficult phoneme that requires a tense, high tongue and a gliding motion of the tongue and lips. It is easier to relax the tongue and substitute a /w/ for the /r/. When this happens, a sentence like, "The rough road was dry," becomes "The wough woad was dwy." The result again is a childish, almost cartoon-character voice.

Additions

Additions also cause problems with pronunciation. Easterners, for example, may suffer from an intrusive /r/ sound. When this happens, "wash" becomes "warsh" and "America" becomes "Americur." Southerners may extend vowel sounds by adding an additional phoneme. One syllable words like "pen," "men," and "an," become two syllables with this addition.

Faulty Articulation

Incorrect production of phonemes is most often associated with a regional accent. Many factors contribute to a regional accent, including where you spent your formative speech years and where your parents are from. If you produce a flat "i" sound by failing to complete the production of the diphthong /aɪ/ in the phrase, "right nice, bright night," for example, you or your language role models may be from certain parts of the South. A nasal /æ/ sound as in "back" (produced by the tongue being too high and tense) will identify you as a Midwesterner or a New Yorker.

In casual speech, regional pronunciations are not incorrect as long as they are within our two accepted regional dialects, Eastern and Southern. As a broadcaster, however, you should adhere to General American pronunciations unless your news director advises otherwise. Many news directors prefer General American speech, as revealed by the 18 percent who indicated in the survey (Appendix A) that regional accents were a problem.

There are some stations, such as country radio stations, that occasionally want a regional sound. There are times when a station will actually train you to speak the dialect of their region. This happened to a friend from Long Island who went to a Texas station. Her first few weeks there were spent learning a Texas accent and eliminating her Long Island sound. If you find yourself in a situation like this, Kenyon and Knott's dictionary, which lists all three accepted dialects, can help you learn a regional accent.

Faulty articulation also involves lisps and excessive sibilance (hissing sound). These problems occur on fricative sounds like /s/ /z/, and /ʃ/ /ʒ/. These phonemes give speakers more trouble with production than any others.

A lisp results from improper placement of the tongue for /s/ and /z/. A frontal lisp produces a "th" sound for /s/ and /z/. Instead of "Suzy sat in the swing," a frontal lisper would say, "Thuzy that in the thwing." Pulling the tongue back will usually alleviate the problem of a frontal lisp.

A bilateral lisp is a harder problem to describe and correct. What happens in its production is that the tip of the tongue makes contact with the alveolar ridge (see Figure 8) and the /s/ or /z/ is produced by the sound going over the sides of the tongue. This is similar to the production of an /l/ phoneme. To correct this, make certain that the sides of the tongue hug the teeth, and the phoneme is produced by friction in the front of the mouth.

Whistling "s" sounds are occasionally a problem for broadcasters. This results from a narrowing of the groove in the tongue through which the air is to escape. Shortening the duration of the /s/ and /z/ phonemes will usually correct this problem.

Excessive sibilance in general can be corrected by shortening the duration of the /s/ and /z/ phonemes. If you feel your sibilant sounds distract from your delivery, try keeping their production light and short.

Focus on Articulation

A) Poor articulation results from omissions, substitutions and additions, and faulty articulation. To understand the effect of omissions, say the following word pairs and note the phoneme omitted in the second word:

center	sinner	/t/
ask	ass	/k/
winter	winner	/t/
picture	pitcher	/k/
field	feel	/d/
painting	paining	/t/
crash	cash	/r/

Notice that omitting the consonant phonemes resulted in a different word being produced.

To experience the /w/ /r/ substitution, say these word pairs:

rag	wag
rate	wait
rock	wok
run	won

B) The tongue plays an important role in the production of vowel phonemes. Say these phonemes, and feel the tongue dropping progressively and the mouth opening as you move down the list (try putting your finger lightly on your tongue to feel this movement):

/i/   as in bee

/ɪ/   as in bit or /u/ as in two

/ɛ/   as in bet or /ʊ/ as in put

/æ/   as in at

/ɑ/   as in spa

C) The /t/ phoneme is usually produced with no voicing and an explosion of air, but there is one exception. In our language, it often sounds overpronounced to use a full /t/ phoneme before a syllabic /l/, /m/, or /n/. Syllabic sounds are produced when consonants form syllables without a full vowel. In these instances, the /t/ may become imploded, or it may sound more like a /d/. Some examples of syllabic sounds preceded by /t/ are:

little	bottom
rattle	button
cattle	mitten
kettle	kitten
bottle	cotton

Articulation Warm-Ups

Forming and shaping sound requires agile articulators and a good ear to monitor pronunciations. If you were training to be a ballet dancer, you would recognize the importance of exercising your body to make it flexible. Warm-ups and stretches would be part of your everyday life. You would also find you needed to practice your dance moves in front of a mirror to continue to improve. As a broadcaster, you should think of your voice in the same way. You are working with muscles, tissue, and ligaments when you are speaking. Your articulators must be as agile as a dancer's body to produce good speech. In addition, just as a dancer practices in front of a mirror, you must monitor your pronunciations to keep them correct.

Warming up our articulators before speech is imperative. Not many of us would walk out our front door and try to run a marathon without stretching our muscles. Stretching brings blood into the muscles which helps them work more effectively.

Do not be embarrassed about doing warm-up exercises. Professional singers and actors know the importance of warm-ups. As a broadcaster, your voice should be prepared prior to on-air work, just as other vocal professionals prepare. By doing warm-ups, you are showing your professionalism.

1) Say these phonemes, exaggerating the mouth positions:

- /ɑ/ as in spa

- /ɔ/ as in caw

- /u/ as in two

- /i/ as in bee

Open the mouth wide for /ɑ/, round the lips for /ɔ/, pull the lips forward in a pucker for the /u/ phoneme, and smile widely for /i/. Continue to say these phonemes in an exaggerated manner, gliding from one to the next. Use this series of phonemes as a warm-up before going on air. After repeating them a dozen times or more in an exaggerated manner you should feel your mouth becoming more flexible.

2) Continuing with the exaggerated stretching from the last Warm-Up, repeat this sentence, extending the vowel phonemes:

- You see Oz.

Pucker the lips tightly for "you." Pull the lips back in a wide smile for "see," and drop the jaw and open wide for "Oz." Repeat this sentence with these exaggerated lip positions as many times as you need to in order to warm-up your articulators.

3) Repeat the following sentences as fast as you can while preserving the consonant plosive formations:

- Put a cup. Put a cup. Put a cup. Put a cup.

- Drink buttermilk. Drink buttermilk. Drink buttermilk.

Rapid repetition of these sentences will help warm-up your tongue. Say these sentences rapidly before on-air work. Be sure you feel air exploding out on the plosive sounds.

4) Chewing and talking at the same time has been used extensively to improve articulation, because chewing loosens the jaw and tongue. To practice this, pretend you have just taken a big bite from an apple and count while you chew. You can also say the months of the year, days of the week, or the alphabet for this Warm-Up. You should exaggerate your chewing while you speak.

5) Ending consonant plosives are difficult to articulate properly. Use the following word lists to practice plosive endings. Hold your hand in front of your mouth and try to feel a burst of air at the end of each word:

Ending Consonant Plosives

/t/	/d/
hit	had
mitt	lad
sit	fad
last	tried
fast	fried
past	filled
laughed	bend
craft	bird

/p/	/b/
top	bob
flop	sob
hop	lob
pipe	web
ripe	grab
deep	curb
seep	stab
leap	tab

/k/	/g/
peak	lag
sneak	hog
freak	frog
slick	log
talk	jog
make	drug
pick	snug

6) For precise broadcast speech, ending consonant plosives must also be formed correctly in sentences. This

involves the same burst of air for each ending consonant plosive that you experienced when you practiced Warm-Up 5. Use the following practice sentences and news copy to improve your ending consonant plosives. Before you begin, mark each ending consonant plosive by underlining, circling, or highlighting. Tape record your reading. Exaggerate the sounds as you say them if you need to. You may sound overpronounced and technical at first. Since these are exercises, do not worry about the technical sound. Continue to practice the sentences and news copy until you can make the delivery more natural while preserving the correct production of the ending consonant plosives.

/t/ /d/
1. West Grand Junction will be hot instead of mild next week.
2. The reporter missed the fight when he jumped from the boat.
3. Word of the shot was called into the station by Rod.
4. The ride was a bad one for the East Coast bird group.
5. In the last game, just one score, Maryland eighty and Washington one hundred.

/p/ /b/
1. A gunman tried to rob the Jog Shop on Curb Street.
2. Pop culture is booming in Deep Creek.
3. Bob will keep a tab on the shop next week.
4. The mob pushed off the curb and toppled the cab.
5. The dog will jump in your lap but the cat will not.

/k/ /g/
1. The West League hit their peak in Lake Placid.
2. Smog will clog the roadways as we dig out from under the snow.

3. The dark will make a rescue effort difficult.
4. The guard will pick up the sleek car at the yard.
5. He will jog the last leg of the race in the dark.

Broadcast Copy to Practice for Ending Plosives

Gunfire shattered the quiet town of Grand Junction in Montgomery County last night. Two men were dead at the scene, another hospitalized following what police suspect was a domestic dispute.

Amtrak officials suspect a faulty rod on the rail line may have made a difficult commute for West bound passengers. Bob Bennett reported that the stop in Westchester County was the result of a break in the rail rod.

In basketball this evening, first in the NBA, it was the Atlanta Hawks over the Washington Bullets one-twenty to one-thirteen. College scores were not as close. It was Memphis State over the University of Maryland ninety-eight to eighty-eight and Stanford beat Georgia Tech in a rout--ninety to forty-eight.

7) Consonant clusters are the most difficult consonants to pronounce. They can be learned by practicing the production of the cluster alone before attempting to incorporate it into words. Repeat clusters alone until you can say them easily and then try the words. This requires very facile articulators. Here are the most common clusters:

Voiceless		**Voiced**	
/ts/	as in bats	/dz/	as in rods
/pt/	as in wrapped	/bd/	as in robbed
/kt/	as in talked	/gd/	as in lagged
/θs/	as in fifths	/ðz/	as in breathes
/sks/	as in desks		
/sts/	as in lists		
/kθ/	as in length and strength		

8) Substitutions often involve the use of /w/ instead of /l/ or /r/. Use these word lists to practice your production of these phonemes. The /w/ is formed by pursing the lips and relaxing the tongue. The /l/ requires the tip of the tongue to make contact with the alveolar ridge or the front teeth. The sound is then allowed to escape from the mouth by dropping the sides of the tongue. The lips can be pulled back for the /l/ sound in practice to make certain they are not pursed as for /w/. Watch your production of these two phonemes in the mirror and be certain the lips are pulled back for /l/. You can force a smile by pulling the lips back for the /l/ in practice to exaggerate the production.

pull	chill
sail	mail
meal	spool
roll	fail

An /r/ requires a gliding movement of the tongue and lips. The lips are pursed at first and then they relax. The tongue is more tense for the production of /r/ than for /w/.

rock	dry
room	pretend
report	travel
dream	around

9) The /t/ /d/ substitution for /θ/ /ð/ involves the tongue being pulled too far back in the mouth. To produce a

correct "th" sound, let the tongue tip come under the upper front teeth, making light contact. Friction should be produced by forcing air through the space between the front teeth and the tongue. To test your production of this, say the following words while watching your mouth in a mirror. You should be able to see your tongue each time you make the "th" phoneme. You might want to begin by lightly biting your tongue tip to position it under your teeth.

Voiceless	**Voiced**
thank	them
thick	the
thigh	than
thorn	they
thrill	that
think	those
ether	then
wealthy	though
nothing	seething
birthday	lather
bath	worthy
path	breathe
mouth	soothe
south	teethe
worth	loathe
faith	weather

A conversational style of storytelling is our preferred method of communicating. The most common problem seems to be reporters walking into the tracking room and reading a script *instead of telling a story about people.*

Terry McElhatton
News Director, KNTV
San Jose, California

Conversation is in . . . we can no longer announce the news to the people . . . they want to hear the news from our announcers the same way they would hear it from a relative across the dinner table.

Dick Heidt
News Director, KFYR–TV
Bismark, North Dakota

Forget that you are "doing the news," and tell your story as if you were talking to one person . . .. *the days of* stiff *news delivery like Jim Dial on TV's "Murphy Brown" are over. Be human when you deliver the news and use inflection to bring the story to life.*

Debbie Bolton
News Director, WAEV–FM
Savannah, Georgia

Enhancing Meaning through Stress and Intonation

There are few topics besides style of delivery that news directors so unanimously agree upon. Appendix A shows that 84 percent of those who responded to our survey marked "Conversational" as the preferred style of delivery. News directors also ranked "Monotone" as the main vocal problem. They emphasized their choice with comments like these:

> "Relax and talk to viewers not at them."

> "The key to good delivery is to make the broadcast sound like a conversation."

> "We want natural-sounding people."

> "Talk to us as if you are telling a story to a friend."

> "Most listeners want people who sound real."

> "Be natural."

"My best advice is simply to relax and tell a story."

Unfortunately, "relaxing and telling a story" is not the easiest thing to do. Many of my clients say that no matter how much they relax, they still sound stiff in the sound booth. It is difficult to read and not sound like you are reading.

A Broadcasting Communication Model

One of the reasons for this difficulty is that most broadcast work is an unnatural communication event. We all know how to use stress and intonation to tell a good story to a friend. Recall the last time you told a colleague about a traffic jam you encountered or an exciting event from your last vacation. Your pitch no doubt went up and down as you talked, and you may have stretched words out to build suspense. You probably got louder to emphasize words, and you may have talked faster to hold interest. In conversation, all of this comes naturally to most of us.

When we talk to someone in conversation, we participate in a communication loop (see Figure 11) that involves sending out a message and receiving feedback from the listener. The feedback we receive may be verbal, with comments like "Really?" or "I see," or it may be a nonverbal nod of the head or a puzzled look. This feedback helps us adjust our delivery to hold the interest of our listener.

Broadcasters in a sound booth, or talking to a camera, work without the help of feedback. The communication loop is truncated (see Figure 11). Messages are sent out, but no feedback exists to help the broadcaster make the subtle adjustments needed in stress and intonation to make the delivery interesting. This is why a monotone or an overdone delivery can happen in the sound booth or when talking to the camera. If

Figure 11
Communication Models

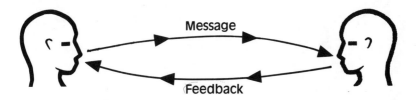

A Normal Communication Interaction

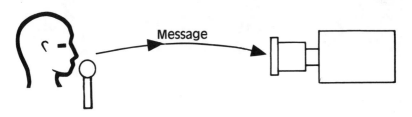

A Broadcasting Interaction

you are looking at your printed copy or the wall in the sound booth, it is difficult to sound natural. Likewise, with the camera as your focal point, the communication loop is not complete.

You may have been advised to imagine you are talking to someone you care about when you read copy. This might involve seeing your mother or a friend when you look at your copy or at the camera. Unless you are good at hallucinating, this is a difficult task. Not many of us can turn a camera lens into someone's face. And even if we can, just seeing the face is not enough. What is really needed is the active feedback that is an integral part of normal conversation.

Much of a reporter's on-air time is spent talking to a camera or a sound booth wall.

Courtesy of KSL–TV, Salt Lake City, UT

Developing A Broadcast Delivery Style

To compensate for the lack of natural delivery, many broadcasters develop a pattern. They realize their delivery sounds flat, so they make an arbitrary choice to stress every third word or every noun or verb. This results in a singsong delivery pattern. Forty-four percent of the news directors responding to the survey said that one of the main delivery problems they hear is the singsong pattern.

Any predictable delivery pattern can distract from the meaning of your copy. If the audience begins to notice your delivery pattern, they have shifted their focus from content to style. Your manner of speaking should never draw more attention than the ideas you are trying to get across to your listener.

In addition, a set delivery style restricts the variation that is needed for different types of stories. Within one news report, an anchor may go from a serious opening story that calls for credibility and concern to a kicker that requires a light delivery. Set delivery patterns do not allow for this kind of variety.

A client recently complained that when she does serious stories she sounds credible, but occasionally she fears she is dull and uninteresting. She compared her normal delivery to Henry Kissinger, who is noted for his understated, monotonous style. For a recent Christmas special, her news director told her to "jazz up" her delivery to fit the mood of the show. Not knowing how to do this, she forced an artificial delivery that she said sounded like a used car commercial. She was changing pitch and rate so much she lost all her credibility and sounded foolish. Without any training in how to change stress and intonation effectively, this can be the result.

Finding Meaning-Laden Words

The first step in developing a process to increase stress and intonation correctly is to find the meaning-laden words in your copy. This assumes, of course, that you do not plan to commit the greatest sin of broadcast delivery, which is to "rip and read" your copy on the air without a practice read-through. Unless you are on the air live during a disaster or a rapidly changing news event, no story should ever be read cold off the news wire or straight from a writer. To rip and read shows a lack of respect for your professional craft and for your audience. Even if a quick read-through is all you have time for before you go on the air, you owe that to your listeners.

Read through your copy out loud (you never help your delivery by reading broadcast copy silently) and look for meaning. On the first read-through you should use a pencil to mark the meaning-laden words. You might want to underline them or circle each one. Meaning-laden words are exactly what the name implies: words that carry meaning. In the sentence, "The quick brown fox jumped over the fence," the words "fox," "jumped," and "fence" carry the meaning. It is nice to know

Reading and marking copy should become routine for all broadcasters.

that the fox was quick and brown, but it is not imperative to the meaning. If you read this sentence with your stress on "quick," "brown," and "over," your listener would no doubt be confused.

I use several examples to illustrate this idea for my clients. One example happens in thousands of homes each night. If I go into my living room at seven o'clock and switch on the television for the evening news, I will most likely then go into the kitchen and begin dinner. I cannot hear every word of the news, but I want to hear the meaning-laden words. If I hear "accident," "Bethesda," and "two injured," my interest will be piqued because I live in the area mentioned. I will go to the television to see the rest of the story.

This example would also be true if I were driving and listening to the radio. I may become distracted by any number of things, but as a broadcaster, you need to pull me into your story by stressing the meaning-laden words.

Another way to think of this concept is to visualize the lighting in a television studio. "Fill" and "key" lighting are two main types used in television. While the fill gives general illumination, the key lighting emphasizes certain people. It pulls those people out from the rest of the set, just as stressing certain words pulls them out from the rest of the sentence.

You can also think of a mountain range. When looking at the range, certain peaks rise above the rest. You see a fairly solid line of mountains with a few peaks standing out. As you read copy and stress the meaning-laden words, you are pulling them out just like the mountain peaks. You are making them stand above the rest by stressing them in a certain way. Your first task, however, is to find these words.

You should read through your copy looking for words that carry meaning. There is no easy formula. The meaning-laden words are not always the nouns and verbs. In this sentence, "Another attack by a pit bull dog has sent an elderly woman to the hospital," the modifiers "pit bull" are important to the meaning. You could find that an adverb is important, such as "continuously" in this sentence: "The gunman was continuously shooting which made any rescue operation impossible." You will usually find that function words do not receive stress. These include prepositions, pronouns, conjunctions, and articles. This is not a hard and fast rule, however. Consider this sentence: "The boy was found in the hole and not beside it." The prepositions "in" and "beside" are important.

A close reading of your copy is the only way to seek out the meaning-laden words. Once you have marked your copy for these words you should have an outline of your story. A robbery story, for example, might give you these meaning-laden words: teenager, shotgun, fast food restaurant, suburban Detroit. Without reading the entire story, you have a good sense of what it says when you read the meaning-laden words.

Pausing for Breath and Meaning

Another initial step in creating a conversational delivery by marking your script involves deciding where you plan to pause.

We have all heard broadcasters who pause at inappropriate places. If the sentence above were divided in this manner, it would lose meaning: "Another attack by a pit / bull dog has sent an elderly woman to the hospital." Many times inappropriate pauses come from the rip and read problem. If you have not read over your copy out loud, you are using guesswork when it comes to pausing. Other times, broadcasters pause inappropriately because they run out of air (see Chapter 1). You should mark your breath pauses so that you do not deplete your air supply as you are reading.

When marking your copy, use a double slash mark to designate a longer pause and a single slash mark for a short catch-breath or a quick pause with no intake of air. Double slash marks are often found at periods and when you go to tape. This is a time when you can take a fairly deep breath. Single slash marks might be found at commas, dashes, ellipses, or at any point where meaning would be helped by a pause.

Marking these pauses before you mark meaning-laden words is preferable if you have the time. This allows you to work with phrases, instead of entire sentences, when you are looking for meaning. A phrase is a group of words between two slash marks. You might have two phrases in this sentence: "Another attack by a pit bull dog / has sent an elderly woman to the hospital." At the slash mark, you would take a catch-breath.

If your copy is written well, you will generally have at least one meaning-laden word in each phrase. In the sentence above you might pull out "attack," "pit bull dog," "woman," and "hospital." Those words carry the essential meaning of the sentence. It is easier to find these words when you work with the short phrases between slash marks.

Ways to Stress Words

Once you have decided where you want to pause and what words carry meaning, you are ready to make some choices about what you plan to do with your voice to pull out your meaning-laden words and verbally underline them for your listener. You will look at each meaning-laden word and decide what you want to do with your voice to stress each word.

You may have heard broadcasters talk about "punching" words to emphasize them. When my clients say they punch words, they usually mean they get louder on those words and possibly go up in pitch. Using this method alone causes problems, however, because it sets up a predictable, singsong delivery. In conversation, we do more with our voice than increase volume and go up in pitch. Incorporating a variety of stress and intonation methods will make your delivery sound more natural and conversational.

Intonation

Use of changes in our pitch in speech is called intonation. We use pitch changes within entire sentences to signal certain meanings, and within words to give them individual significance.

There are two basic patterns of intonation we use for sentences. Our normal intonation pattern calls for us to go down in pitch at the ends of sentences. This includes questions that begin with an interrogative (how, when, where, which, what, who, whose, whom, why). If you say, "How are you?" you go down in pitch at the end of the question. Try saying this sentence, listening to your pitch: "I had a good time." If you said it as a statement, you went down in pitch on "time" to indicate a complete thought. Now say it as a question: "I had a good time?" You should notice that since there was no interrogative to indicate a question, you went up in pitch on "time." Rising intonation in our language indicates a yes-no question or suggests uncertainty, insecurity, doubt, hesitancy, or an incomplete thought.

We also use pitch changes within sentences on certain words, and this is what is important for the process you will use to mark your script. Generally, in our language, for the most emphasized word in any phrase, our voices go up in pitch. Once you know your meaning-laden words, you should look at each one and decide if a pitch change would be an appropriate way to stress that word, and what pitch change is best.

There are three ways to use pitch for specific words. You can go up in pitch as you did in the above question without an interrogative, and you can go down in pitch as you do at the end of most sentences. Going down in pitch usually indicates finality or seriousness. If you say, "Three persons were killed in the accident," you would most likely go down in pitch on "killed." A sentence such as, "There were two survivors of the accident," would require a choice on your part. "Two survivors" could either go up or down in pitch, and either would be effective.

You can also use a circumflex intonation, which means you go up-down-up on a word or down-up-down. In our language, this intonation pattern indicates doubt or suspicion. Say this sentence and practice the circumflex intonation on the word "refused": "The CEO refused to be interviewed by our reporter." By alternating your pitch on "refused" you can indicate that something suspicious is going on with this executive.

When using a pitch change, you can glide up in pitch or you can step up. A glide up means that you begin the word at the same pitch as the previous word, but you go up in pitch as you say the word. A step up involves a clean pitch change from one word to the next (see Phonation Warm-Ups 7–10 in Chapter 2).

Duration

We also vary the length of words and syllables to stress them. If you said, "It was the biggest ice cream soda I ever ate," you probably stretched out the word "biggest." Stretching words out gives them more significance. This technique is very effective for numbers and figures. If a huge crowd turned out for a rally, you might say, "There was a record attendance of twenty-thousand people." Saying "twenty-thousand" slowly will impress the listener with the number.

Speeding up our speech can be effective as well. In the sentence, "The trial suffered still another set-back," it would be effective to speed up "still another set-back." You could also slow it down to make a point that the trial is dragging on. The choice would be up to you. Try saying this sentence both ways and see which sounds better to you.

Using variations in duration to emphasize certain words can be just as effective as variations in pitch. Changes in pitch or duration of words makes your meaning-laden words stand out from the rest, which helps your listener understand your story.

Volume

If you remember the last time you were angry about something, it may be easy to recall what an increase in volume is like. You may have said, "I said no!" On the word "no," you probably raised your volume.

For some broadcasters, increasing volume is their primary way of stressing words. These are the broadcasters who are difficult to listen to for any length of time. You feel as if you are being shouted at instead of reported to when this becomes a pattern.

Increasing volume is a legitimate way to stress words, but it should be used judiciously. It puts stress on your listener and on your throat. To increase your volume, you use more tension in the larynx. And this tension can lead to any number of vocal problems, as discussed in Chapter 2.

Pausing for Stress

In addition to pausing for meaning, you can also use pauses for stress. Pausing before and after a word or phrase pulls out an idea for the listener. It is as if the idea is suspended from the rest of the sentence. This might be used for a parenthetical phrase or clause such as, "The defendant, who is accused on ten counts, was not in the courtroom." It is natural to pause before "who" and after "counts."

You can use this method of pausing in other instances as well. You might say, "The county has a / restrictive limit / on new construction." By pausing in this way, the phrase "restrictive limit," is stressed.

A Method for Marking Scripts

Using the techniques described above (pitch, duration, volume changes, and pauses) you now have a basic method to improve stress and intonation in your broadcast copy. These techniques provide a way to superimpose a natural, conversational delivery on a very artificial process. You will be able to verbally underline your meaning-laden words for your listener just as you do in normal conversation.

This process can be used to mark every piece of copy you are given to read. Figure 12 outlines how the method can be used. The copy marking method as presented here is only a starting point, however, for what should become a personal shorthand for you. In Figure 13 you see how this method looks when used on copy. I tell clients I hope that if I saw their copy a year after they worked through this method with me I would not recognize their markings. You should streamline the method to fit your needs.

It is important to remember as you go through the marking process, that any story can be marked in a number of different ways and still be effective. There is no set way to mark each story. While I might choose to stretch out the phrase "Ten Most Wanted" in the last sentence in Figure 13, you might want to go down in pitch. The choice is a personal one, but the important thing is to verbally underline the meaning-laden words by using a stress and intonation technique.

It is easy to use this method with copy for the sound booth as well as for Teleprompter copy that is hand fed into the machine. Unfortunately, the method cannot be used with most computer-generated Teleprompter copy. I have not found a computer program that allows for this marking system. Hopefully, in the future such a program will be developed. If you have a computer-generated Teleprompter, you may have to rely on spaces, dashes, and other typing techniques to develop a marking system.

Broadcast Copy Preparation Method for Stress and Intonation

This procedure may seem tedious and technical at first, but with practice, you will devise your own shorthand markings. The process can be integrated into the read-through of your copy.

Marking Teleprompter copy aids delivery.

Courtesy of KSL–TV, Salt Lake City, UT

Always perform the following procedure *in pencil* on your copy since you may find that you want to change markings:

1) Read through the copy out loud to check for difficult words.
   A. Look up the pronunciation of any difficult words.
   B. Write the phonetic transcription of difficult words on your copy.

2) Mark major breath pauses with // and minor breath pauses or pauses without an air intake with /.

3) Select the *meaning-laden* words to stress. Mark stressed words (usually at least one in each phrase) with the appropriate symbol given in Figure 12. (A phrase is a group of words between breath pauses.)

4) Reread copy out loud to check stress pattern.

5) Practice copy out loud as many times as possible.

When you begin working with this method, you should stick to the approach given here. As you progress with it, you will develop a personal marking method that will be much faster. You will find that the marking method is very tedious at first. It might take you thirty minutes to mark one page of copy. The usual response I get from clients is that there is no way this can ever work with the deadlines of a normal day.

Any new process is very technical at first. Remember when you first learned to drive a car? You may have thought that process would never be comfortable. What my clients find is that the more they practice this method of marking their script for meaning, the faster it becomes. Practice should be done

---

Figure 12
Vocal Methods for Stressing Words

1. Inflection up   The court has refused to vote.

2. Inflection down   The court has refused to vote.

3. Circumflex   The court has refused to vote.
   inflection*

4. Increase in volume   The court has refused to vote.

5. Pausing before &   The court has /refused/ to vote.
   after word

6. Stretching the   The court has refused to vote.
   word out**

7. Saying the word   The court has refused to vote.
   faster

*In American speech, circumflex inflection indicates doubt or suspicion.

**This is especially effective for numbers to give them added significance.

---

initially in your non-work hours (see Stress and Intonation Warm-Ups). Do not expect to be able to read through this chapter and begin marking your on-air copy the same day.

I always caution clients against trying to use a marking method immediately. One anchor at a top market did not listen

---

Figure 13
Sample Broadcast Copy Marked for Delivery

Three-thousand people in the Washington,

D.C., area were notified they had won two

free tickets to the Redskins' football

game.// About 100 of them showed up today at

the Convention Center for the tickets and a

pre-game brunch,/ but they were thrown for a

loss: // U.S. marshals and police sprang their

trap and arrested them all as fugitives.//

Some were wanted for burglary, robbery or

murder.// Two of those caught in the sting

were on the local list of /Ten Most Wanted.//

Reprinted with permission from *Writing Broadcast News,* Mervin Block, Bonus Books, Inc., 1987.

---

to my warning and almost lost her job when she tried to learn the method on the air. Her news director called her in and wanted to know what had happened. She was stumbling over words and sounded awful. This may be the result if you rush this process.

You should spend weeks, even months, getting comfortable with a marking process. Once you are comfortable with it, you will hear tremendous improvement. The client whose delivery for a Christmas special sounded like a used car commercial found this method gave her the confidence to abandon her monotone. She could use her voice to enhance meaning with the knowledge that she was emphasizing the correct words. For her, the method became part of her routine almost immediately, and she was using it on the air after practicing only a few weeks.

Examples of Script Marking Methods

Personalized marking methods have been used by both novice and veteran broadcasters for years. Edward R. Murrow had a personal marking style, which is illustrated in the news lead below, provided by one of his former writers, Ed Bliss (see Figure 14). Bliss relates how Murrow always used a #2 yellow pencil to mark his script before each radio broadcast of "Edward R. Murrow—The News" (1947–1959). Bliss reports that Murrow would spend around ten minutes marking and rehearsing a six minute news summary. Bliss explains that Murrow used the exaggerated commas shown in Figure 14 as slash marks ". . . to feed the people a fact at a time." Regular commas indicated a slight pause. Murrow also often used a

Figure 14
Edward R. Murrow Copy

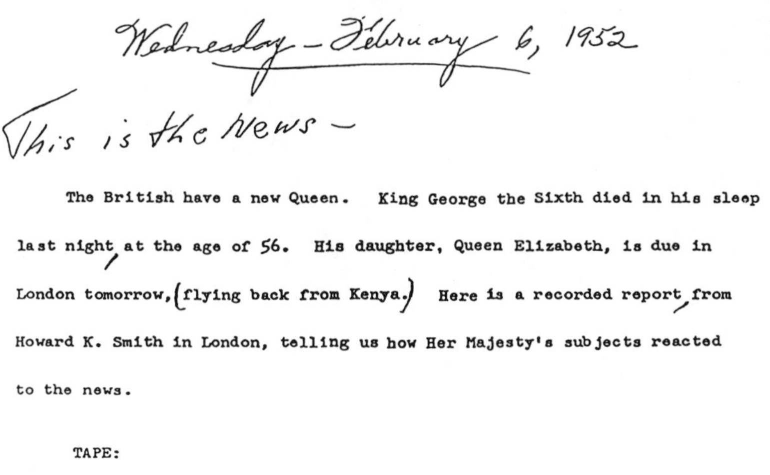

Wednesday—February 6, 1952

This is the News —

The British have a new Queen. King George the Sixth died in his sleep last night at the age of 56. His daughter, Queen Elizabeth, is due in London tomorrow, (flying back from Kenya.) Here is a recorded report from Howard K. Smith in London, telling us how Her Majesty's subjects reacted to the news.

TAPE:

Courtesy of Ed Bliss and Mrs. Edward R. Murrow

Edward R. Murrow in wartime London where his coverage began with the effective use of a pause: "This . . . is London."

pause before verbs that he wished to emphasize. He used parentheses to set off phrases for meaning as well as underlining for emphasis. Murrow made few editorial changes in his scripts, according to Bliss, but he spent his preparation time deciding how to use his voice to enhance the meaning of the copy.

Brian Olson, News Director, KGWN–TV in Cheyenne, Wyoming, teaches his staff a marking method that uses symbols in a different way (see Figure 15). Olson explains:

> Nothing fancy about the markings really. The key words are underlined for emphasis. The stronger the line, the stronger the emphasis. Ditto for pauses. More "dots" . . . . a longer pause. What makes it all work is subtlety. The best changes in inflection and tone are always the subtle ones.
>
> Other tips: For on-air work, always be on-set at least ten minutes before air. This allows you to relax, take a few sips of water and read through your copy at least twice. And read it aloud! So many anchors read their copy to themselves, then fumble all over the place when they get on the air.
>
> Note that in this copy, we used the phonetic spelling of Gurnard (Gurh-nard). If there is the remotest chance of mispronunciation, always "spell it out!"
>
> So I suggest subtlety and relaxation mixed with a large dose of "out loud" preparation. This is always a successful mix.

You can see that the markings used at KGWN are much more streamlined than the ones presented in Figure 12. Like Murrow's markings, they have been refined into a system that is fast and efficient. Your marking method should evolve as well. At first it will seem slow and technical to perform, and your delivery will sound slow and technical as well. As you continue to practice the technique, however, your own system and style will emerge.

Figure 15
Brian Olson Copy

NEWSOURCE EXTRA 2-14-90 10p bdo	IMAGINE...
VTR EXTRA/MONITOR.............	LIVING AND WORKING
	IN A STEEL TUBE..
	~~_LESS_~~ THAN THREE
	HUNDRED FEET LONG..
	LESS THAN FORTY
	FEET WIDE.
	WITH YOU ARE
	ONE HUNDRED ~~~~ AND FIFTY
	OTHER PEOPLE.
	THERE ARE NO WINDOWS
	AND NO SUNLIGHT....
	AND NO FRESH AIR
	FOR PERIODS OF UP
	TO THREE MONTHS
	OR MORE.
	THIS IS WHAT
	LIFE IS LIKE
	ABOARD A NUCLEAR
	ATTACK SUBMARINE.
	TONIGHT IN PART
	TWO OF HIS SPECIAL
	ASSIGNMENT
DISSOLVE FULL SCREEN CONT SIL	NEWSOURCE EXTRA
	SERIES..."AMERICA'S
	SILENT ~~~~ SERVICE"...
	BRIAN OLSON SHOWS
	US WHAT IT'S LIKE
	TO WORK AND LIVE
	ABOARD ~~~~
	THE GURH-NARD...

Courtesy of Brian Olson, News Director, KGWN-TV, Cheyenne, WY

Effective Use of Rate for Broadcast Delivery

Rate is an area that many broadcasters find confusing. They feel they deliver their copy too slowly, and when they speed up they get too fast. This is a common area of concern, because rate is very difficult to monitor on your own. I recently told a client to double her rate as she read a story for me. She thought that was ridiculous advice until she listened to the recording of her delivery at the faster rate. What had been a plodding delivery and a dull story suddenly became interesting.

Our rate of speaking is determined in many ways by our speech models. If your parents talk rapidly, you will most likely talk rapidly. If you come from a large family where you had to talk fast to be heard, you will have a rapid rate. On the other hand, a quiet, calm childhood may have produced a slow rate of speaking.

In broadcasting, control of rate is important, and reveals your sense of involvement and interest in a story. In your private life, it is acceptable to answer the phone with a slow, low-energy voice if you feel bad. For broadcasting, you must not let your moods show in your delivery. If you feel bad, you have to cover it up with a consistent rate and the sense of involvement that comes through marking your copy for meaning.

Appropriate Rates

Normally we read out loud at between 145 and 180 words per minute (wpm). The most comfortable speed is around 150 to 175 wpm (to learn your rate see Focus on Stress and Intonation). Our speaking rate is somewhat slower than our reading rate. Most of us speak at around 160 wpm or less. This is probably because we use more pauses and stretch words out more when we are talking. One contradiction to this is certain radio formats that call for very rapid-fire, extemporaneous delivery. In these instances, radio deejays may talk at 200 wpm or more.

When broadcasting, you can use rate to help verbally emphasize the mood of your story (see Table 2). A serious, sad

Table 2
Rate Continuum

145 wpm	160 wpm	180 wpm
Material that is		
SAD	EXPOSITORY	LIGHT
SERIOUS	DESCRIPTIVE	HAPPY
GRAVE	UNEMOTIONAL	HUMOROUS
TECHNICAL		
COMPLICATED		

story would be read more slowly than a kicker. Adjusting your rate makes the mood of the piece clearer for your listener.

It is often helpful to make a note in the margin of your copy that indicates the mood of each story. One client told me she likes to put the mood at the bottom of the page preceding each story. In this way, she can adjust her mood and rate as she turns her page of copy. It is all too easy to begin a sad story with a rapid rate before you realize the gravity of the piece. It is hard to adjust your rate and mood after you have begun a story.

Components of Rate

Pauses have a great deal to do with overall rate. Two important components of rate are the number of pauses and the length of pauses. If you mark your pauses with slash marks, you will be able to gauge the number of pauses. The more you pause, the slower your delivery rate will be.

Another factor of rate that is more difficult to monitor is the duration of syllables. We vary the rate of syllable production based on the importance of the word and our natural speech pattern. Speech in a Southern accent is considered slow because Southerners tend to give more duration to their vowel sounds. By stretching out the vowels, the rate slows down. A Northerner or Midwesterner might clip the vowel sounds, which would speed up their speech. Tape recording your delivery and monitoring the duration of syllables will help you become aware of your syllable production.

By marking your script, you can also monitor the words and phrases that you have decided to stretch out for meaning. If you find in a page of copy you are stretching out six or eight words, you will know that the delivery rate will be slow.

Focus on Stress and Intonation

Here is a summary of the main points involving stress and intonation for broadcast speech.

1. Most broadcast delivery is done in an artificial environment that eliminates feedback from the communication situation.

2. In normal speech, we use variations in pitch, rate, duration, and pauses to make our speech interesting and to reinforce meaning.

3. Our pitch goes down at the ends of sentences that are statements and in questions that begin with interrogatives.

4. Our pitch goes up at the ends of yes-no questions because there is no interrogative to signal the question. Going up in pitch also suggests uncertainty, insecurity, doubt, hesitancy, or an incomplete thought.

5. For broadcast speech, we can use variations in pitch, rate, duration, and pauses to give this artificial situation a natural sound.

6. Normal broadcast speech rate when reading copy ranges from 145 to 180 wpm. Rate should be adjusted to reinforce mood.

A) It is sometimes difficult for an individual to gauge the amount of stress and intonation used in broadcast work. For this reason, it is a good idea to tape record yourself reading some copy and ask a friend, a voice coach or teacher, or your news director to review the tape with you. Often when we think our pitch is rising, it is too subtle for others to detect. If this is the case, refer to the Phonation Warm-ups for ways to improve your pitch variation (see Chapter 2). Likewise, a loud volume to us may seem soft to someone else. Volume must be judged by a listener. Tape record this story using your normal broadcast delivery and review it with a critic you have selected:

```
A new study says children who
become hooked on television at an
early age often become teenagers
who are overweight. And the study
by two Boston doctors reports that
the more time these teens spend
watching T-V, the more weight they
put on--making them truly heavy
viewers.
```

Reprinted with permission from *Writing Broadcast News*, Mervin Block, Bonus Books, Inc., 1987.

B) Rate is also a difficult component of delivery to monitor without a conscious effort. The AP wire copy given below has a double slash mark at 150 words. Single slash marks indicate groups of ten words before and after the 150 mark. Read this section at your normal rate, timing your delivery. Mark the point you reach after reading for exactly sixty seconds. Next, count up or back from the 150 mark to where you stopped reading to calculate how many words per minute you read. If you find you were reading as slowly as 140 wpm, reread the section, trying to speed up. If you read above 180 wpm, try to slow down. This is an unemotional story that should be read with a normal delivery of around 150 to 175 wpm.

A prisoner being taken by federal marshals from Alabama to California, bolted out of a moving plane's emergency exit after landing on Saturday and fled into the darkness, authorities said.

U.S. Marshal Stuart Earnest said the escapee, 44-year-old Reginald D. Still, was en route from a federal hospital in Talladega, Alabama, to Sacramento, California, where he was scheduled to go on trial on a charge of interstate transportation of a stolen motor vehicle.

Earnest said the plane contained 44 prisoners when it touched down at Will Rogers World Airport. No other prisoners tried to escape, he said.

Still wearing handcuffs and shackles, he leaped out of the plane's emergency exit, onto a wing and then the tarmac as the plane was braking, / the marshal said.

One of the eight security people on / the plane jumped out to chase the escapee, Earnest said.//

Federal marshals and local, county and state authorities fanned out / across the airport property, southwest of Oklahoma City, in the / search.

Prisoners are normally transported by a Boeing 727, but a backup, a

```
Convair 580 propeller, was being
used Saturday because the jet was
being repaired, authorities said.
    The U.S. marshal's service
routinely transports prisoners
every other day to courts and
penitentiaries around the country.
The transportation program is based
in Oklahoma City, and prisoners on
overnight trips often are housed
overnight at a federal correctional
facility in El Reno, 30 miles west
of here.
```

Reprinted with permission from *Writing Broadcast News,* Mervin Block, Bonus
Books Inc., 1987.

C) To feel the effect of no feedback on communication,
look just above someone's head when you are talking or turn
and face the wall. Ask the person not to respond verbally while
you tell them about an interesting event. You will notice that
without feedback, natural conversational delivery is impaired.
Many people feel the same way when talking on the telephone
because they are not making eye contact with their listener.

Stress and Intonation Warm-Ups

Discovering that your stress and intonation is not appropriate
and deciding to change it is not always enough. You must know
how to change stress and intonation to enhance meaning. The
method described in Figure 12 gives you a way to do this.

When you first begin practicing this method, it will seem
time-consuming and technical. For the method to work, you must
continue to practice until you feel comfortable using the method
and your delivery sounds natural and conversational. Practice
every day, marking copy and tape recording your delivery.

Keep in mind that this method is based in meaning, and is not simply a technique or a delivery trick. If you have decided where your meaning-laden words are, you need not fear that you will fall into a set delivery pattern. Every story will be different based on the meaning. You will be reading for sense and not for sound. You should be able to develop a delivery that does not sound forced or insincere.

Remember also that there are many ways each sentence can be marked. The important thing is to pull out the meaning-laden words for your listener. Where you decide to pause and how you decide to stress a word or phrase is a personal decision that should be based in meaning and your delivery style.

1) In each of the following sentences, go through the marking method as described in Figure 12. First mark pauses if there are any, and then find the meaning-laden words. Once you have selected the words, decide how you plan to stress each one and mark each with the appropriate symbol.

- Two men are dead and a third in

  stable condition after a multiple

  shooting in Gainesville last night.

- Authorities are still

  investigating a robbery in the

  southeast part of the city this

  morning.

- The Shelby County Mental Health

  Association will provide trained

  counselors to help locate

available housing for the

homeless this winter.

- 19 of 30 people sought in

  connection with the large scale

  cocaine ring, which operated out

  of the Pizza Shop on west Main,

  were arrested last night.

- A commuter aircraft on final

  approach and a private plane

  collided over the Knoxville

  airport this afternoon injuring

  ten people.

2) Once you have practiced the marking method on sentences, expand your practice to include complete stories. The UPI wire stories given below and in Appendix E provide practice material.

Cries of joy sounded into the night
in South Africa, where black
nationalist leader Nelson Mandela
is set to be freed Sunday. But
authorities report eight people
were killed and 45 injured near
Johannesburg, when police fired to

break up blacks hurling stones and
gasoline bombs. South African
President de Klerk says the
government is committed to a new
constitution which is fair to all
blacks and whites.

As some of the 400-thousand-
gallon oil spill laps the shore of
Huntington Beach, California, the
government is about to cite a
cleanup contractor for using
improper clothing. The Occupational
Safety and Health Administration
says it will cite Chempro of Long
Beach for letting workers wear
sneakers instead of oil-resistant
boots. The government agency also
says the company did NOT give some
workers enough training in cleaning
up Wednesday's spill.

Police in Las Cruces, New Mexico,
are circulating sketches of suspects
in a bowling alley robbery in which
four people were killed. At least
two gunmen forced seven people into

an office of the bowling alley
Saturday and opened fire. The four
fatalities included an alley
employee, his daughters aged seven
and two, and a 13-year-old girl.
Three people were wounded. The
robbers set fire to the office.

Secretary of State Baker is
threatening to with-hold U-S aid to
Bulgaria if the government there
does NOT work to ensure free and
fair elections. Baker travelled to
Sofia Saturday to express doubts
about the Communist government's
preparations for the elections.
Those doubts included muzzling of
the press. The United States has
proposed 300-Million dollars in aid
for Eastern Europe in 1991,
excluding Poland and Hungary.

James ``Buster''Douglas closed one
of Mike Tyson's eyes and then turned
out his lights, with a knock-out to
take the heavy weight championship
of the world. Sunday's fight in

Tokyo was expected to be a mere
tuneup for Tyson for another fight.
Tyson knocked Douglas down in the
eighth round but the challenger
came back. Douglas was ahead or tied
on all the score cards by the time
he ended the bout with an uppercut.

Words are our business. We must not only use them correctly in print, but pronounce them correctly as well. Communication is an art, if you do it properly. You have to work at it, and never take it for granted.

Keith Silver
News Director, WWLP–TV
Springfield, Massachusetts

The delivery must be clear, with no hurdles for the listener to overcome. A flawlessly delivered newscast is one of the only ways you have of making sure the listener hears what you are saying, instead of focusing on the mistakes, stumbles, etc.

Lynn Levine
News Director, WWNZ
Orlando, Florida

Stumbling Blocks— Commonly Mispronounced Words

Correct pronunciation of words is a constant challenge for broadcasters. In addition to the problems of omissions, substitutions, additions, and faulty articulation discussed in Chapter 4, there are other problems that arise.

We have all enjoyed watching bloopers by newscasters. *Spoonerisms*, or reversals of sounds in two words, are often the most humorous. "Show you to your seat," becomes "Sew you to your sheet," as a spoonerism.

Another problem called *metathesis* involves the reversal of sounds in a word. Metathesis would change "nuclear" to "nucular" and "ask" to "aks."

Haplology is the omission of a repeated sound or syllable. If this is a problem for a speaker, you might hear "govner" instead of "governor" or "twenty" instead of "twenty."

The pronunciation list that follows is meant to be a beginning for what should be your personalized list of commonly mispronounced words. You might want to photocopy this list and begin a personal file of your own problem pronunciations. You should customize the list by adding words that are particularly troubling for you. These might include local names and pronunciations, as well as general words. For local pronunciations, check with your news director. Your station should have a policy for regionalisms, such as the Kansas use of a /θ/ ("th") ending in the word "drought," instead of /t/.

As you see, in the list that follows, the correct pronunciations are not given. Just like your spelling teacher in grade school may have told you, the only way to learn a word is to look it up yourself.

It is a good idea to check pronunciations in two dictionaries. This is time consuming, but once you have looked up all the words, you have a list to practice throughout your career.

If you look through the list and feel you pronounce most words correctly, be wary. Most speakers think they are saying these words correctly, but they are all commonly mispronounced. You may be omitting sounds such as the plosives in numbers like "eighty" and "ninety." Additions may sneak into words like "athlete" resulting in "athelete." Or you may be reversing sounds or mispronouncing phonemes. Developing the practice of looking words up in a dictionary is important.

Here is a list of recommended dictionaries:

The American Heritage Dictionary. 2d college ed. Boston: Houghton Mifflin Company, 1985.

Ehrlich, Eugene, and Raymond Hand, Jr. *NBC Handbook of Pronunciation*. 4th ed. New York: Harper & Row, 1984.

Kenyon, John Samuel, and Thomas Albert Knott. *A Pronouncing Dictionary of American English*. Springfield: Merriam-Webster Inc., 1953.

The Random House Dictionary of the English Language. 2d ed, unabridged. New York: Random House, 1987.

Webster's Ninth New Collegiate Dictionary. Springfield: Merriam-Webster Inc. 1985.

Two other interesting sources are:

Elster, Charles Harrington. *There Is No Zoo in Zoology and Other Beastly Mispronunciations*. New York: Macmillan Publishing Company, 1988.

Urdang, Laurence, ed. *The New York Times Everyday Reader's Dictionary of Misunderstood, Misused, and Mispronounced Words*. Revised Edition. New York: New American Library, 1985.

100 Commonly Mispronounced Words

Correct Pronunciation

ABERRANT _____

ACADEMIA _____

ACCESSORY _____

ACCLIMATE _____

ACCOMPANIST _____

ADMIRABLE _____

AFFLUENCE _____

ALLEGED _____

APARTHEID _____

APPLICABLE _____

ARCHETYPE _____

ASBESTOS _____

ASSEMBLY _____

ASSUAGE _____

ATHLETE _____

ATMOSPHERIC _____

AUXILIARY _____

BARBITURATE _____

BEQUEATH _____

BULIMIA _____

BYZANTINE _____

CALM _____

CAPRICIOUS _____

CARIBBEAN _____

CAVEAT _____

CLIQUE _____

COMPARABLE _____

CONSORTIUM _____

CONTEMPLATIVE _____

CONTROVERSIAL _____

DAIS   _____

DATE   _____

DECIBEL   _____

DELUGE   _____

DISPARATE   _____

DUTY   _____

ELECTORAL   _____

ENVELOPE   _____

ENVOY   _____

ERR   _____

FACADE   _____

FORMIDABLE   _____

FORTE   _____

FOYER   _____

FUNGI   _____

GALA   _____

GENUINE   _____

GOVERNMENT   _____

GRIEVOUS   _____

HARASS   _____

HEINOUS   _____

HERB   _____

HOMICIDE   _____

HOSPITABLE   _____

IDEA   _____

ILLUSTRATIVE   _____

IRREPARABLE   _____

IRREVOCABLE   _____

JEWELRY   _____

JUROR   _____

LAMBASTE   _____

LENGTH (STRENGTH)   _____

LIAISON   _____

LIBRARY   _____

LONG-LIVED (SHORT-LIVED)   _____

MEASURE   _____

MEMORABILIA   _____

MISCHIEVOUS   _____

MORES   _____

NAIVETE   _____

NEGOTIATE   _____

NUCLEAR   _____

OFFICIAL   _____

OFTEN   _____

OPHTHALMOLOGIST   _____

PALM   _____

PENALIZE   _____

PIANIST   _____

POINSETTIA   _____

PREFERABLE   _____

PRESTIGIOUS   _____

PRIVILEGE   _____

PROGRAM   _____

REALTOR   _____

REPARTEE   _____

SANDWICH   _____

SCHIZOPHRENIA   _____

SIMILAR   _____

SPECIES   _____

SPONTANEITY   _____

STATUS   _____

SUCCINCT   _____

SUPPOSED   _____

THEATER   _____

TOWARD   _____

TRANSIENT   _____

VASE   _____

VEGETABLE   _____

VENEREAL   _____

ZOOLOGY   _____

Personal Pronunciation List

Difficult Word   **Correct Pronunciation**

_____   _____

_____   _____

_____   _____

_____   _____

_____   _____

_____   _____

_____   _____

Difficult Word	Correct Pronunciation
_____	_____
_____	_____
_____	_____
_____	_____
_____	_____
_____	_____
_____	_____
_____	_____
_____	_____
_____	_____
_____	_____
_____	_____
_____	_____
_____	_____
_____	_____
_____	_____
_____	_____

Difficult Word	Correct Pronunciation
_____	_____
_____	_____
_____	_____
_____	_____
_____	_____
_____	_____
_____	_____
_____	_____
_____	_____
_____	_____
_____	_____
_____	_____
_____	_____
_____	_____
_____	_____
_____	_____
_____	_____

Difficult Word	Correct Pronunciation
_____	_____
_____	_____
_____	_____
_____	_____
_____	_____

Questionnaire Statistics

Broadcast voice is important to radio and television news directors in this country. A questionnaire for this book sent to 671 radio and television news directors confirms this interest.

When considering doing this survey, I was advised that it is difficult to get news directors to respond to questionnaires that are mailed to them. I was told to expect a maximum of 10 returns from the list of 671 names. The questionnaires were mailed on January 5, 1990, and three weeks later I had received 197 responses (29 percent). Even though 29 percent is not a large enough response for a statistically valid study, it does provide enough data to draw interesting conclusions. The returns represented all parts of the country, and indicate radio and television news directors' interest in voice, and their desire to express their feelings on this issue. The comments found in Appendix B further reveal the concern many news directors have about the lack of emphasis placed on voice training.

Figure 16 is the questionnaire that was sent, asking what news directors look for in broadcast voice, as well as how they feel about the importance of voice.

Figure 16

QUESTIONNAIRE - *BROADCAST VOICE HANDBOOK by Ann S. Utterback, Ph.D.*
Publishers: Bonus Books and RTNDA (September 1990)

1. When evaluating on-air talent, do you consider voice to be (circle)

   Very Important   **Important**   **Not Very Important**

2. Has voice been a factor in your hiring or firing of on-air talent?

   Yes   No

3. Do you have on-air talent at your station now who you feel could improve their vocal delivery?

   Yes   No

4. What type of delivery do you like? (You may circle more than one.)

   Conversational   Credible   Precise   Authoritative

   Other _____

5. What's the major voice or delivery problem you've encountered in your staff? (You may circle more than one.)

   Nasality   Overpronounced   Breathy   Nonauthoritative   Monotone

   Too High-Pitched   Too Low-Pitched   Sloppy Articulation

   Thin Quality   Singsong   Limited Range   Regional Accent

   Other _____

6. What **COMMENTS** or advice concerning voice or delivery do you have for the readers of *BROADCAST VOICE HANDBOOK?* (continue on back)

Name (Please Print) _____

Title _____   Station _____

Address _____

If you prefer your name NOT to be published, please check here
Return form to: Ann S. Utterback, Ph.D.   _____
                  11415 Empire Lane
                  N. Bethesda, MD 20852

The returns were broken down as follows:

52 Radio News Directors

145 Television News Directors

_____

197 Total Responses

The first three questions brought almost complete agreement from both radio and television news directors (see Tables 3–5). An overwhelming majority agree that voice is either very important or important in evaluating on-air talent (see Table 3, radio and television). Ninety percent of radio news directors and 89 percent of television news directors also report that voice has been a factor in their hiring or firing procedures (see Table 4, radio and television). Currently, 99 percent feel that

Table 3

When evaluating on-air talent, do you consider voice to be

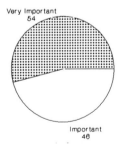

Very Important 54

Important 48

Not Very Important (0%)

Radio Percentages

Very Important 54

Not Very Important 1

Important 45

Television Percentages

Table 4

Has voice been a factor in your hiring or firing of on-air talent?

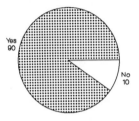

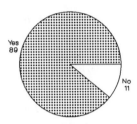

Radio Percentages   Television Percentages

Table 5

Do you have on-air talent at your station now who you feel could improve their vocal delivery?

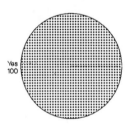

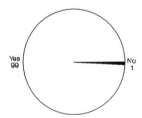

Radio Percentages   Television Percentages

someone on their staff could benefit from voice training (see Table 5, radio and television).

When asked what type of delivery they like, radio and television news directors again agree (see Table 6). Conversational delivery is foremost (84 percent combined) with a credible and authoritative voice also desired (71 percent and 42 percent combined). A precise delivery is not as important as a conversational sound (17 percent combined). News directors also added the following categories as types of deliveries they look for: Radio—interesting, sense of concern, versatility: Television —engaging, sounds interested, excited, correct diction and inflection, warm, trustworthy, pleasant, friendly, personable, seemingly natural.

The most variation came in certain responses to question number 5. When asked the major voice problems they have encountered, radio and television news directors differ the most on voice qualities such as pitch. Forty percent of radio news directors think that voices that are too low-pitched are a major problem. Only 3 percent of television news directors agree (see

Table 6
Type of delivery preferred

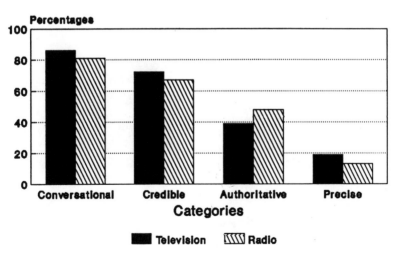

Table 7). Voices that are too high-pitched are of greater concern to television news directors than radio (15 percent radio, 28 percent television).

Television news directors also appear to have more difficulty with thin voices (see Table 8). Thirty-one percent of television news directors marked this category, compared to 23 percent for radio.

Aspects of stress and intonation such as a singsong delivery and a nonauthoritative sound also differ between radio and television. Radio news directors are looking for a more authoritative sound while television news directors seem to be more concerned with the singsong quality of some deliveries (see Table 9).

Radio news directors seem to be more tolerant of regional accents. They also are not as concerned as television news directors with an overpronounced sound (see Table 10).

Radio and television news directors agree on many of

Table 7

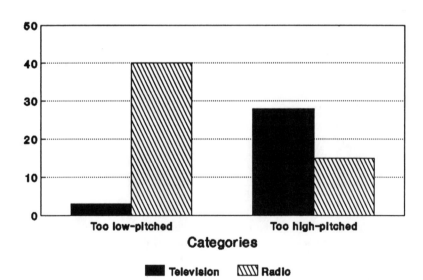

Table 8

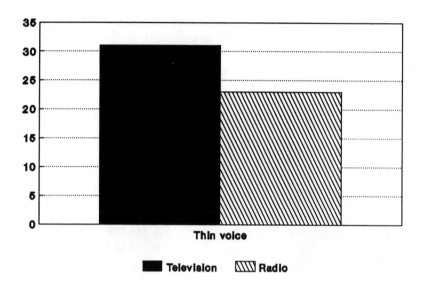

the delivery problems that they have encountered. Table 11 gives all the categories and their percentages.

News directors added many categories to encompass the problems they hear from their staff. Radio—stumbling, too fast, put-on quality ("Ron Radio" voice): Television—lisp, unnatural delivery, poor breathing, not conversational, sibilance, stiff, staccato, overpowering, choppy, punching delivery, not enough interpretation, overauthoritative, forced, no variety, poor pacing.

Conclusions

The responses to this survey indicate the interest radio and television news directors have in broadcast voice. They also reveal that radio and television news directors perceive most voice problems as the same for both media. When asked what major delivery problems they have encountered, radio and television news directors responded within 10 percentage points on 7 of the 12 categories. They agreed almost completely on the type of delivery they like (conversational).

Table 9

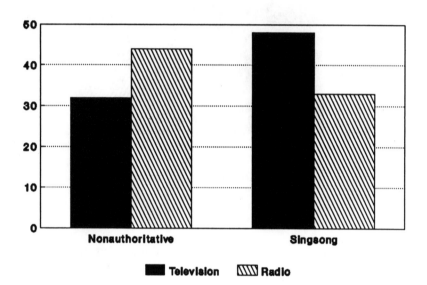

Table 10

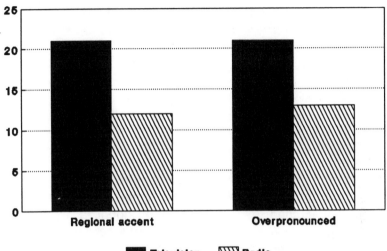

Regional accent — Overpronounced

Television   Radio

Table 11
Question #5 Responses with Percentages

	RADIO (%)	TELEVISION (%)
Nasality	25	31
Overpronounced	13	21
Breathy	13	14
Nonauthoritative	44	32
Monotone	52	45
Too High-Pitched	15	28
Too Low-Pitched	40	3
Sloppy Articulation	46	45
Thin Quality	23	31
Singsong	33	48
Limited Range	29	30
Regional Accent	12	21

Table 12
Priority Ranking of Voice Problems

RADIO	%	TELEVISION	%
Monotone	52	Singsong	48
Sloppy Articulation	46	Monotone	45
Nonauthoritative	44	Sloppy Articulation	45
Too Low-Pitched	40	Nonauthoritative	32
Singsong	33	Nasality	31
Limited Range	29	Thin Quality	31
Nasality	25	Limited Range	30
Thin Quality	23	Too High-Pitched	28
Too High-Pitched	15	Overpronounced	21
Breathy	13	Regional Accent	21
Overpronounced	13	Breathy	14
Regional Accent	12	Too Low-Pitched	3

Comments from News Directors

What better way is there for you, as an on-air broadcaster, or someone who wants to go on-air, to learn news directors' views on voice than to hear them direct from the source? This section gives you an opportunity to do just that.

The last section of the questionnaire mailed to 671 news directors asked, "What comments or advice concerning voice or delivery do you have for the readers of *BROADCAST VOICE HANDBOOK*?" Following are the 124 responses to that question (Television = 84, Radio = 40).

I was delighted and amazed at the variety of responses and length of some of these comments. You will notice that the comments come from small and large radio and television stations from all parts of the country. This material has been very helpful in my research for this book, and you have seen many of these comments used as chapter headings throughout the book.

No titles are given here because all of the people who responded were either news directors or acting in that capacity (vice president for broadcasting, etc.). The responses are arranged by state, city, and call letters. When the person asked not to be identified, only the city and state are given.

ALABAMA

I like to get a TV News candidate who has had several years of Radio News background because I feel it improves their breathing, voice quality, and delivery.

Birmingham, WBMG-TV, Al Crouch

Good voice quality is every bit as important as a broadcaster's writing style. Even the best written copy has far less impact when the delivery isn't right.

Huntsville, WAAY-TV, Cliff Windham

I believe the most effective human communication is "one on one" conversation. The effective anchor must be able to deliver the message as if he or she were talking to one person. Therefore I believe that a natural style rather than affected "deep tones" is the best way to communicate in the "one on one" style.

Montgomery, WAKA, Jon Mangum

ARKANSAS

Diaphragmatic breathing is a must in broadcasting . . . too many people come out of school and have never heard of it!

Little Rock, KTHV-TV, John Rehrauer

CALIFORNIA

The major problem with younger staff is that "somebody" tells them they need to sound "authoritative" since they look "young." Well, hell they are young! By trying to sound "authoritative" they start to strain their voice and make it thin and nasal. I have to "relax" their style back to what it was when they were hired.

Bakersfield, KERO-TV, Walt Brown

Careful! Voice "quality" is highly subjective. Personality in a voice, including non-standard pacing and "regionalisms" are becoming more desirable.

Los Angeles, KFWB, Ken Beck

Don't try to sound like the network people. Sound like people. This is the first and greatest commandment.

Sacramento, KOVR, Mike Ferring

I try to hire reporters and anchors who talk to people in conversational style—rather than "deliver." I have worked with a dozen people over my twenty years in news, who had great voices—but bad attitudes—or lacked the intelligence, drive and insight to do this job properly. In all but the worst cases—I'll take brains and ability over voice any time.

San Francisco, KNBR, Mark Provost

Voice is more than pitch and articulation. It is physical and psychological. Beginning broadcasters should work with professionals who can help in these areas as well.

San Francisco, TV

I'd advise your readers not to try to use a broadcast voice (or, rather, what they think is a broadcast voice) for on-air work. Unless a reporter is very talented, that kind of delivery comes off as faked and unnatural. Much better, I think, to use the natural voice as a point of departure for on-air work, and infuse it with a slightly larger quality through inflection and word emphasis.

San Francisco, KQED–FM, Anne Marshall

A conversational style of storytelling is our preferred method of communicating. The most common problem seems to be reporters walking into the tracking room and *reading a script* instead of telling a story about people. Often even our best writers drag down their copy by trivializing it verbally . . . or not emphasizing the right key words to give the impact the story needs and deserves. The best communicators in our newsroom are reporters with a radio background who know how to tell stories and don't underestimate the power of their voice and delivery in getting the viewer emotionally involved or excited about the story. 95% of TV news reporting is voice-over. Competent and compelling story tellers are the people we look for, people who can not only write to video but can hold the audience with the power of their voice.

San Jose, KNTV, Terry McElhatton

COLORADO

Use a sense of restrained urgency in your voice. Get listeners to feel you are interested in what you have to say. It makes them interested enough to pay attention.

Denver, Radio

CONNECTICUT

If someone is just getting started, such as a student, I tell them to take a speech class. I also advise (and remind) people that in Broadcast Journalism, you are writing for the ear, not the eye—so read it out loud to hear what it sounds like. Proper breathing is also important to a good delivery.

New Haven, Radio

It is more important to be understandable than to sound like "Joe-anchor person."

West Hartford, TV

DELAWARE

Don't try to make your voice something it's not. Work to improve it within its range. Be natural. The worst mistake is to put on a "radio" voice instead of a natural delivery.

Wilmington, WDEL, Don Voltz

The biggest concern is a voice which is too fast in delivery and "forced." Too many young reporters sound like they work too hard at making their voice sound authoritative. Also, the drop off at the end of a sentence which creates a singsong sound is prevalent in applicants.

Wilmington, WHYY–TV, Nancy Karibjanian

DISTRICT OF COLUMBIA

A broadcast voice should be trained, controlled and modulated to the point that you are aware not of the voice but of the information that is being delivered.

Washington, D.C., CNN, Bill Headline

Voice in a news story should not be noticed. If it is, something is wrong.

Washington, D.C., Cox Broadcasting, Andy Cassells

It is very difficult to improve one's delivery by reading a book. It entails reading aloud to a coach who can listen and suggest improvements.

Washington, D.C., Newslink/WIN, Rob Downey

In certain periods of the day people watch/listen to TV news as they do something else. A strong and pleasant authoritative voice helps to keep them focused on the station and the news being delivered.

Washington, D.C., TV

Reporters do not place enough emphasis on the voice. Often they do not realize how much impact the voice has on the communicative ability of the story.

Students do not have a good understanding of when accents are acceptable or not acceptable. Often, they express interest in trying to get rid of an accent but don't know how to go about it or don't have the necessary dedication.

The voice is the #1 detriment to good delivery. Its effect is immediate and overpowering. No amount of excellent writing or good on-air presence can compensate for a poor voice. It is the #1 detractor of good delivery.

Washington, D.C., Washington Independent Productions, Susan Stolov

We want natural-sounding people—not people stamped into a cookie-cutter style—which means every on-air reporter must develop his/her own personal flair and style—but be himself/herself—consistently. And I respectfully suggest people listen to TV reporters with their eyes closed to appreciate the value of a strong radio presence.

Washington, D.C., Radio

FLORIDA

I look for reporters with a background in radio. They generally have a much better delivery because they have had to rely on their voice alone in telling their story to the viewer. People with just TV experience rely on the pictures and don't place enough emphasis on voice. A great delivery coupled with great pictures makes for a GREAT story.

Miami, WPLG–TV, Michael Sechrist

I tell beginning reporters to find a voice model . . . someone in the industry whose presentation they can learn from. Until a reporter/anchor has an idea of what they want to sound like, it's difficult for them to develop a style.

Orlando, WDBO, Marsha Taylor

The delivery must be clear, with no hurdles for the listener to overcome. A flawlessly delivered newscast is one of the only ways you have of making sure the listener hears what you are saying, instead of focusing on the mistakes, stumbles, accent, . . . etc.

Orlando, WWNZ, Lynn Levine

The notion that deep voices are better is a myth. Research clearly shows this rates very low on the list of reasons why people like announcers.

Tampa, WFLZ/WFLA, Gabe Hobbs

1. Good (proper) inflection.
2. Don't read too fast.
3. Learn how to let the listener know you're going from one thought to another without telling them.

West Palm Beach, WJNO/WRMF, Jim Edwards

GEORGIA

Too much emphasis has been placed on "booming pipes" in radio. Radio announcers should talk like people talk.

Atlanta, WSB, Lee Hall

If it appears it's unlikely that voice problems can be overcome —suggest another role in the broadcast news business.

Macon, TV

Don't forget to breathe! And tell the story, don't read it! Forget that you are "doing the news," and tell your story as if you were talking to one person in the listening audience . . . the days of stiff news delivery like Jim Dial on TV's "Murphy Brown" are over, be human when you deliver the news and use inflection to bring the story to life.

Savannah, WAEV–FM, Debbie Bolton

The viewer decides quickly whether to accept an anchor. The appearance and vocal quality are the criteria used first to help them decide.

Savannah, WTOC–TV, Larry Lyle

No viewer wants to be announced to—they wish to be part of a conversation. The on-air talent who can be an effective conversationalist reaps the highest rewards . . . money!

Savannah, WTOC–TV, Doug Weathers

IDAHO

Suggestion for work on articulation . . . read Dr. Seuss books aloud . . . he wrote some real tongue-twisters!

Pocatello, KPVI, Dan Hovel

ILLINOIS

There is nothing magic about a good broadcast voice. Good vocal delivery is often as much the result of hard work and following the right advice as it is God-given talent.

The best vocal deliveries are not automatically the booming, resonant recitations that laymen often associate with the notion of good broadcast voices. In television, the medium is sufficiently multidimensional that people who make good use of average voices can do very well. In fact, I feel they make up the lion's share of the talent in this industry.

In my experience, proper breathing and phrasing are the main stumbling blocks to a good delivery. Part of this comes from not understanding the story, even if the reporter has written it. But some of it also comes from not knowing how to make the story and the individual understood. In other words, the reporter may understand the story but use of his/her voice is a roadblock to convincing the viewer of that.

One way I help young people to work around this problem is to get them to mark their copy on the words that need to be emphasized. Inflection goes a long way toward credibility.

Another thing I work on with them (after the fact) is to make certain words, phrases and sentences are written in such a way as to allow for best use of the voice. Eliminate certain clauses and the rest of the clutter, etc.

I do not work with people on general voice quality. I do suggest to them this is a professional coach's job, and I don't want to be party to them doing something that will screw up their voices. Bad advice can get a person sued.

Champaign, WICD, Jack Keefe

Ann Utterback is excellent at showing young, inexperienced reporters how to improve their delivery. I use her frequently to help train my students in using their voice properly. The response has been extremely favorable. Her techniques are easy to use and practical. Long after you have heard Ann in person or read her work you can use her techniques.

Evanston, Medill News Service, Lou Prato

My best advice is simply to relax and tell a story. Too often I get airchecks from people who are forcing their voices beyond their natural ranges. Simplifying writing helps make a delivery more natural as well. Think about the kind of words and phrases you use. If they would not come naturally in everyday speech—don't use them.

Mokena, Satellite Music Network, Diane Kepley

I think voice is a very important career development issue too many broadcasters pay too little attention to.

Far too many of today's young broadcasters never get much of a chance to develop their voice or style of delivery, because they don't get the necessary practice. They graduate from college, get a job as a TV reporter, and at the most, read about a minute's worth of copy per day in a package for the evening news. Unlike most equipment a broadcaster uses, a voice gets better the more it is used. That's why those who grew up in radio and switched to television generally have much better voices (deeper, more authoritative, more relaxed and conversational) than those who have worked only for television.

A good voice does not make a good reporter, but a bad voice can ruin a good reporter's chances for success in broadcasting. I have seen very good reporters passed up for anchor jobs because no one would want to listen to them for an entire newscast.

There is also no excuse for having a bad voice, unless one has a physical impairment that affects his or her voice. With a minimal amount of expert advice and a maximum amount of use, any voice can and will improve.

For the most part, however, you will have to practice on your own time. Make copies of the days' newscast and read it out loud, into a tape recorder. Play it back. Listen for things you don't like, and read it again. Do this for a half-hour a day, five days a week, for six months, and your voice (and delivery) will improve more during that time than it would over a five-year period if you do nothing more than a general assignment TV reporter is required to do.

Here's another hint. Get about five minutes of copy together, and team up with another broadcaster who is also working on developing his/her voice. Split up the copy, and take turns reading stories. (You should be taping this.) After you have read the news, discuss it for another five minutes. Play it back and critique yourself. You will probably find you were too stiff while you were reading and too sloppy with your enunciation while you were discussing it. Your goal should be to merge the two styles, so eventually you can both read and discuss the news in an articulate, but conversational, style. This will help you immeasurably in the event you one day become a TV anchorperson who is expected to have on-air conversations with your co-anchors.

If a news director tells you your voice doesn't matter much, he/she is either a bad news director or he/she wants you to remain a general assignment reporter for the rest of your professional life.

A clear, pleasant, articulate, authoritative, and conversational voice is the quickest ticket any good broadcast reporter can have to good jobs and promotions.

Bad reporters should forget everything I've said and look for another profession.

Quincy, WGEM–TV, Ralph Bristol

INDIANA

While new reporters need to work on their reporting and newswriting skills, they must not forget to work on delivery. Before I ever applied for my first radio news job, I practiced with a tape recorder. When I stopped laughing at what I heard, I went for the job.

If you haven't spent years listening to radio newscasts and watching network news on television, do that! See how the newscasters who've made it, do it. Learn from them and develop a style that is conversational.

Here's some quick advice that is not entirely my own:
1.) Write news in short, one-thought sentences.
2.) On radio, treat the mike as if it was someone's ear.
3.) On television, read as if you were speaking to one person.

4.) Don't announce. Announcer is a job title. Speak.
5.) Relax. Tension does all kinds of bad things to your voice.

Fort Wayne, WANE-TV, Bill Wagman

I wish anyone going to school to be an on-air personality would first have a voice instructor evaluate their voice and the use of it and give advice on what should be worked on in preparation for applying for a job in radio or television.

Fort Wayne, TV

Learn proper breathing (and writing that accommodates it . . . run on sentences make for bad delivery).

Delivering with authority so that the viewer believes you know what you are talking about is another problem area. I see a lot of young people here who don't quite understand this until they are worked with.

When I see a tape from an individual who has a bad voice I ask them if this is the kind of voice and delivery they regularly hear from successful people in the business. If it's not, I tell them what to work on.

Fort Wayne, WPTA, Wayne Ludkey

Don't become pedantic and at the same time don't get "sloppy" with your words . . . be natural . . . be yourself . . . don't imitate . . . project . . . (that doesn't mean shout—one can project in a conversational tone).

Indianapolis, Radio

You only have one opportunity to get your message across to the public—if they don't understand (or get bored listening to a lackluster delivery) there are other channels to watch.

Indianapolis, WTHR-TV, Bob Campbell

IOWA

Dealing with many entry-level reporters I find the main thing they need to do is relax and be themselves. Often they try to overdo it, trying to project false enthusiasm or energy.

Mason City, KIMT–TV, Doug Merbach

KANSAS

If viewers don't understand your anchors, regardless of their news talents, they will tune-you-out.

Topeka, WIBW–TV, Jim Hollis

I always look at reporting skills, writing technique, and ability to get along with people when I hire someone. But in radio news the most important aspect is on-air delivery. It's "the final product."

Wichita, KFDI AM/FM, Dan Dillon

KENTUCKY

Voice quality, or lack of same, is the responsibility of the talent.
FOR STUDENTS, vocal problems should be addressed early in their training. If a student has not reached an acceptable level of vocal performance by their senior year, they should be

advised to follow a course that would put them off-camera (production, assignment, editing, videography). I'm a little more than irritated at Broadcast Schools that take tuition from students and then cut them loose to be disappointed by news directors.

FOR EXISTING PROFESSIONALS looking for a job change, ask for professional advice and cure the problem before you send out the resume tapes.

No news director will hire a problem. There are too many available professionals without problems.

Louisville, WDRB–TV, Hal Stopfel

I've found from both personal experience and from hiring talent . . . especially young people . . . have not developed their own style of delivery. The most natural (and successful) announcers often come from radio where they've had the opportunity to develop their style (experiment, change, etc.). Young broadcasters should copy successful styles from solid professionals . . . then combine them into their own personal style.

Paducah, WPSD–TV, Terry E. Reeves

LOUISIANA

The ability to develop control of one's voice is vital to becoming a success in broadcasting. I have seen many advance far beyond their other abilities simply because they learned how to use their voice, and likewise, I have seen the opposite apply. The voice is the dominant salable commodity in broadcasting, and therefore, cannot be taken lightly.

Alexandria, KLAX–TV, Stan Wyatt

The key to good delivery is to make your broadcast sound like a conversation. This is a special mix. A delivery must be easy to listen to yet authoritative enough to be credible.

Baton Rouge, WBRZ–TV, Rick Willis

Communication and Broadcast Journalism students should be required to take more speech classes.

New Orleans, TV

MARYLAND

While one's voice is important, it does not have to be heavy for a male or rich for a female. A lighter voice, if presented with a credible style can overcome most voice problems.

The proper use of the voice is paramount and is probably one of the most overlooked areas in college training.

Regional accents are the least acceptable voice/speech problem in this area of the country. "Bawlamerease" is unacceptable in this market.

Baltimore, WBAL, Bob Shilling

Less and less often we're seeing a deep, rich voice as a primary consideration for hiring in this industry. That doesn't mean News Directors take lightly the idea of voice quality—to the contrary. We're now trying to get the most out of what would have been considered "marginal" voices only a few years ago. My major obstacle in working with younger anchors and reporters has been to get them to stop "pretending" they're something or someone they're not. When one fakes or forces authority it comes off so poorly. A viewer isn't fooled—only bothered.

Salisbury, WMDT–TV, Ray Carter

MASSACHUSETTS

The days of eliminating people from consideration for on-air jobs because they lack a big, booming voice are behind us. Excellent writing and a professional, personable delivery can overcome even minor voice problems. It's the total "package" that counts.

Boston, Radio

Proper phrasing, combined with a conversational writing style, can do more to create an authoritative, credible sound (i.e., no b-s, here's the straight story) than almost any other approach.

Boston, Radio

The vast majority of applicants have had little or no professional voice training. As a result, they lack proper breathing techniques, and never achieve the voice potential they have. Very few know how to breathe from the diaphragm.

As for advice, take all the Journalism and related courses you want . . . but . . . take the time to learn how to use your voice properly.

Boston, WHDH-Radio, Joe Morgan

Talk, don't speak.

You're not Miss America giving a speech about saving the world—you're talking to people in their homes.

Springfield, WGGB-TV, Roger Ball

Words are our business. We must not only use them correctly in print, but pronounce them correctly as well. Communication is an art, if you do it properly. You have to work at it, and never take it for granted.

Springfield, WWLP-TV, Keith Silver

MINNESOTA

Broadcast journalists should realize that voice is a tool of communication. It can affect viewers' perceptions of a story. Reporters and anchors should take a much more active approach to improving their voices. It is probably the most ignored of all broadcasting tools. It shouldn't be.

Minneapolis, KMSP–TV, Penny Parrish

Be natural.
Be believable.
Know what you are reading; don't just read words, communicate the ideas, concepts and feelings behind the words.

Minneapolis, Radio

MISSISSIPPI

Being able to project yourself without it sounding as such, is very important. This requires precise breath control with the simple ability to communicate. Being able to display confidence without being pretentious, some knowledge on most subjects, hearing while listening, and the ability to convey your thoughts in an intelligent fashion and with a fluid delivery is extremely important for anyone aspiring to be the future broadcaster of tomorrow.

Jackson, WLBT–TV, Dennis C. Smith

Speak conversationally and that means to write conversationally.

Tupelo, WTVA, Terry Smith

MISSOURI

Be yourself and use your own voice and inflections. Too often, new people try to be someone else. They must be themselves, and talk as if they were telling the story to a friend. In this way, they will use the proper emphasis and stress the points they would want to make to a friend.

Use a tape recorder to capture general conversation, then analyze the delivery of others and yourself. Use this style while on microphone.

When writing stories, write for the ear and not the eye. It may read well but sound bad.

Jefferson City, KRCG–TV, Roger E. Wellman

Broadcast schools/college Journalism programs should devote more time to teaching good broadcast delivery. Too many people seeking entry-level positions have inferior deliveries.

Voice instructors should *not* try to improve newscasters by trying to make their voices deeper. Credible, conversational deliveries are much more important than deep voices.

Springfield, KTTS–Radio, Dan Shelley

The importance of voice quality cannot be over-emphasized. An award-winning reporter may never get recognized if viewers can't stand to listen to more than two lines of copy!

Springfield, KYTV, Marci Burdick

MONTANA

It continues to amaze me that colleges and universities continue to graduate students destined for broadcast positions who have sub-standard communication and presentation skills.

Many schools offer courses in something called "Speech," but they seem to emphasize writing and preparing speeches, not delivering the final product.

As a small market news director, I receive dozens of applications each year from young graduates looking for their first full time reporting position. I am appalled by the number who won't make the cut because of some delivery problem . . . or a combination of delivery problems.

I don't care if a student graduated Cum Laude from an Ivy League school; if they have a thick regional or ethnic accent or a thin or plodding delivery, they won't be offered any on-air position here . . . or at most broadcast stations.

The regional or ethnic accent may be the most important to attack. Viewers and listeners will question the credibility of someone who obviously doesn't sound like they are from "around here." For example, I believe Boston, New York City and heavy Texas accents just don't play well outside those limited geographic areas.

Less difficult to fix, and far more common in my experience, are people with underdeveloped voices. They tend to breathe in the wrong place, or have a monotone or singsong delivery. I also find most don't know how to use their vocal range effectively.

Sometimes these problems are worked out by the individual due just to time-in-grade. On occasion, they are lucky enough to find themselves in a position to get professional help from a talent coach or speech teacher. Some never overcome this handicap. It hurts their chances for promotion.

Members of my staff are able to get occasional coaching from talent specialists with our consultant. I also send a couple staff members to regular sessions with a professor from a local college, to help them hone their skills. It's that important . . . even in the 164th market.

Billings, KTVQ–TV, Al Nash

Beginners should do a lot of watching and listening. Pay close attention to radio and television broadcasters who are good, not to copy their particular style but to get an idea about delivery. Everyone should develop his or her own style of delivery but individual initiative is very important, rather than waiting for a news director or voice coach to try to show you the way. This is an area that seems to be ignored, or treated too lightly at many schools.

Great Falls, KFBB–TV, Dick Pompa

NEBRASKA

Some thoughts on "voice" . . .

1. When I put an anchor's audition tape on, the first element in my evaluation of the talent is "voice." Do they "sound right." I am not as concerned about specific qualities as I am concerned about "distractions." Is there something about the voice that causes me to notice it and to be distracted from what they are saying?

For a reporter, I am not as concerned about voice as I am with an anchor, unless the voice is really a distraction. Maybe it is because a reporter is not on the air for as long or because I am also watching video. Or maybe it is because the reporters I have known who possessed what some might call "poor voices" were excellent storytellers and used television well.

2. A concern I have is the number of audition tapes from college students with serious voice problems. Print journalists are taught to type. Why aren't broadcast journalists taught to "speak" properly? The voice of a television journalist is a "tool" and the journalist should learn how to use it properly just like learning how to use a camera and how to edit.

3. I hear a lot of young anchors reading every story in a newscast the same way. I think every story has a mood and tone and the anchor's delivery should reflect that mood. I think it is something young anchors should think about, and be taught; how to develop the skill of changing moods during a newscast.

Lincoln, KOLN–KGIN, John Denney

It seems that our education system has forgotten the power of voice. We don't teach people how to use and improve their voices in school. Often by the time they get through college and their first two jobs, it is almost too late. It's great to be a good journalist but if the voice is bad the audience won't want to listen.

Omaha, KMTV, Loren Tobia

NEW JERSEY

Build on the basics—practice what you can through air check evaluations. Be yourself. Be relaxed. Speak with, not at, the audience. Let writing reflect your voice. Lastly, breathe!

Asbury Park, WJLK–WJLK–FM, Shawn Marsh

Don't ignore voice-impairing illnesses. This is one of the biggest problems I encounter with employees. They won't admit that they are stressing their voices, and often spreading disease to others in the newsroom. Take a day off and give everyone a chance to stay healthy.

I have found that most radio news people don't realize how fragile their voices can be, until they lose their voice. The recovery time is typically much longer than expected.

Toms River, WOBM FM/AM, Carolynn Jones

NEW MEXICO

While voice quality is no longer critically important to success in broadcast journalism, effective verbal presentation is. A person who is difficult to understand or to listen to is not an effective communicator.

Albuquerque, KGGM-TV, John McKean

NEW YORK

I feel broadcasters take the matter of voice for granted. New people especially must work harder and with more attention to how they present their material. We must never forget that it is our voice only that gives the listener an image, if you will! We must gain the listeners' respect and trigger their imagination!

Buffalo, WGR, Ray Marks

Be yourself.
False, pushed delivery sounds just like that. Such qualities destroy rapport with the audience. Voice is fine, but the biggest problem here is writing skills.

New York, CBS Radio, Larry D. Cooper

It's more important to work on your writing than your voice or looks, but that said, I think a good voice is one with personality.

New York, MTV Networks, Linda Corradina

Think about what you are reading, communicate with thought and conviction.

New York, TV

1. Careful of "fast" delivery . . . items run together.
2. Keep it simple . . . use everyday language.
3. Air check yourself . . . I have been in broadcast 43 years—I still air check! And be yourself!

New York, WNEW-AM, Mike Prelee

Job applicants at my TV station need to be more concerned about using their voice as a tool. Using the dramatic pause and a wider vocal range. It is why I have always looked at applicants with some kind of experience in radio.

Plattsburgh, WPTZ–TV, Stewart Ledbetter

NORTH CAROLINA

Tape a newscast and let a news director comment on your delivery. This should be no later than the beginning of the junior year!

Raleigh, WPTF–AM, Mike Blackman

I believe one of the most important points students aspiring to become broadcasters fail to realize is that they must become excellent readers. If you do that well, in most cases, voice training is possible. It's not always important to have what we in the profession call "deep pipes," if you can read well and express yourself to the viewer or listener, a deep voice is not the key to getting that elusive radio or TV job.

Raleigh, WRAL–FM and the North Carolina News Network, Shedd Johnson

NORTH DAKOTA

Conversational is in. We can no longer announce the news to the people. They want to hear the news from our announcers the same way they would hear it from a relative across the dinner table.

This is all complicated, of course, by the fact that while they want us to be conversational, they also want us to come across as authoritative and professional. Talent today must be a jack-of-many-styles.

Bismark, KFYR–TV, Dick Heidt

If you read your story like you think it's interesting and important, the listeners are more likely to think so, too.

Fargo, KTHI–TV, Charley Johnson

1) Speak with a natural voice, non-affected delivery.
2) Breathe from the diaphragm.
3) Strengthen your voice by singing.
4) Don't fool around and misuse your voice in trying to be comical. It can be permanently damaged.

Fargo, KXJB–TV, Dave Hoglin

There is a very special balance that needs to be struck in your delivery between being conversational, credible, authoritative, friendly and natural.

Fargo, WDAY–TV, Al Aamodt

OHIO

Although times have changed, "voice" is still the main ingredient in my hiring method. What good is twelve years of college if the newsperson sounds like a teenager with influenza? Some years back we radio types listened for deep, super-authoritative voices, but that has changed. Now-a-days a person with a good, solid, interesting voice can make the grade . . . but he or she had best be able to get 100% flexibility out of what voice they have.

Additionally, there's an element of "show biz" or "acting" that a person must develop. That can be explained as "style/believability/confidence" rolled into one.

I don't mean to suggest that a person should "fake it." I mean most of us have never met Gorbachev in person. Yet, newspeople must go on the air and sound as if they know all there is to know about Gorbachev, foreign affairs, the KGB, etc. We rarely have personal knowledge of the persons and places involved in some national, and certainly international stories. But for the listener, we must sound convincing. They need to believe we had lunch with Gorby at Burger King last week. That's the kind of credibility and authority to shoot for at least. I am not saying we ever lie to the audience. I only paint this confident style as a goal. I want a news anchor who can say "the sky is green" and be believed. The integrity must also be there to make the journalist well balanced. Great delivery with no morals or integrity makes for an egocentric jerk!

Cincinnati, WKRC–AM, Richard Hunt

Probably my best advice is to tape yourself . . . review the tape for yourself . . . and then, ask a qualified broadcast professional for his or her observations.

When someone does give you advice . . . listen closely to what they are saying . . . solicit several opinions and find out if they have a common criticism. If they do, listen to your tapes again . . . if you hear it, act on it.

I like to encourage beginners to find someone whose broadcast style they like listening to . . . and emulate it. Later on, of course, once you get the basics down . . . branch out and develop your own unique way of delivering a story, through excellent writing and creative delivery.

Cincinnati, WLW–Radio, Kathy Lehr

Within a newscast, from story to story, vary the pace, but keep it quick to achieve a conversational style.

Cleveland, WERE, Vivian Goodman

TV news does not require overly powerful voices. Rather, voices need to be comfortable for the listener. Authority, credibility, and trust, along with good articulation need to be combined with a conversational delivery.

Cleveland, WUAB–TV, Dan Acklen

I think a good newscaster has the ability to "see" a story as they read it—that is, they are able to add the inflection, emotion, and character to their delivery, just as if they were standing in front of an event doing a play-by-play. This takes a certain degree of experience and imagination. It also requires a person to step out from behind the social barriers we erect around us. You have to let the you come through in your delivery. If all we wanted was the facts, ma'am, and nothing but the facts, we could read a paper or watch a teletype. People listen to the radio not only to be informed, but to be entertained, stimulated, and connected to a larger world. They want to hear people—not automatons conversing with them.

Columbus, WTVN–AM, Dave Claborn

OREGON

Voice quality is certainly an important part of our business, but, in my opinion, even more important is reading with understanding. Too many people read words with no idea of the overall meaning of what they are reading. Viewers and listeners have only one shot at knowing what we are trying to communicate. It has to be delivered in a pleasant, straightforward manner with a pleasant, well modulated voice. A nasal, high pitched, unpleasant voice can be an instant turn-off and we may never get a chance to make our point.

Eugene, KVAL–TV, John H. Doyle

It is important to realize how your voice and the tone in that voice affect people—not just over the air but in person, around the office, and with sources.

If you sound like you know what you're talking about, people will believe you do!

Medford, KTVL–TV, Gayle Mitchell

Don't force the voice. It could be damaging.

Portland, KATU–TV, Ron Miller

As audiences get older—understandable delivery will become more important. We often forget that we are in the communication business and that means effective basic oral communication.

Portland, KGW, Phil Wenstrand

PENNSYLVANIA

Project. Breathe. Don't take yourself too seriously.

Harrisburg, WHP AM–FM, Chris Fickes

The best advice for young people getting started is to work in radio. Radio has traditionally been the place that separates those with good voices from those with bad voices. Since fewer young people want to consider radio first, they must have a similar experience in their college work. Since job applicants outnumber the available jobs, stations will be selective about the people they hire. Those with poorer voices will be left behind.

For everyone in broadcasting, practice, practice, practice! Read out loud to your kids or to yourself. Then if things still have not greatly improved in your voice, seek professional help.

Lebanon, WLYH–TV, Clifton D. Eshbach

The single recommendation I make to on-air talent is to develop an appropriate range in their voice. Different assignments require different tones of voice.

Philadelphia, Group W Newsfeed, Terry O'Reilly

People should cut their tracks as if they're talking on the phone. Write and speak in more of a conversational tone.

Philadelphia, KYW–TV, Steve Schwaid

SOUTH CAROLINA

One doesn't have to be blessed with a perfect voice to do well in broadcasting anymore. Reporters and anchors should simply be able to do a little "storytelling" . . . to be comfortable for viewers to watch and hear. Network anchors Brokaw and Jennings do a terrific job of "storytelling."

Charleston, TV

Few young interns are prepared to read well. Even those who had courses in this do not do well as a whole. We have had theater majors, or some with a drama background, do better than journalism grads. These drama folks, though, can't write. I consider voice preparation as essential as typing and basic newswriting. It should be learned already when someone comes into a newsroom.

Columbia, South Carolina ETV, Tom Fowler

I hire entry-level or second-job reporters. I've noted a tremendous weakness with delivery. Recently, I had a reporter-candidate with a Master's Degree from a major journalism school. She was willing to come to work for entry-level money and certainly had the credentials, but her delivery just wasn't good enough for me. I suggested she get a job as a radio reporter or anchor and work on her delivery every day. I gave her specific pointers, the most important of which was to listen to her tapes at home at night. Four months later, she had improved to the point that I hired her, and I'm very satisfied with her. I have another similar candidate to whom I made the same suggestion. She called recently to tell me she's accepted a radio job and is working hard on her voice and delivery. This is an important and very overlooked topic!

Florence, WPDE–TV, Timothy P. Kenny

SOUTH DAKOTA

When evaluating on-air talent I think voice is important only because it must convey a conversational style, be credible, precise and authoritative. The need for deep, resonant baritone sounds is long since past. Most broadcasters want people who sound real.

Sioux Falls, KDLT–TV, Steve Snyder

TENNESSEE

No matter how poor the quality of a voice it can be improved with hard work to an acceptable quality.

Johnson City, TV

Too many television reporters are more concerned about their appearances than their voices. Certainly, appearance is important—but so is delivery.

So much can be accomplished in terms of effective communication through the use of good vocal technique. Authority, credibility and emotion are just some of the images that are conveyed through voice.

It isn't necessary to have a "big" voice . . . but it is necessary to learn how to best use the voice you have.

Nashville, WTVF, Mike Cavender

TEXAS

Reading a news story so the viewer/listener will understand it, is not as easy as it sounds. Being conversational does not mean being sloppy or regionalistic. It takes constant work and study to make the audience listen to what is said, not who is saying it. The job of a communicator is to make it sound easy to do, even though it isn't.

Abilene, KTAB-TV, Bob Bartlett

When they are voicing something, they should really think about what they're saying. Put themselves in the place where the story occurred. That way, they'll sound as if they really know what they're talking about, as if they're really telling someone about the story.

Austin, KVUE-TV, Carole Kneeland

Writing affects voice. Short sentences with a single thought are much easier to punch for emphasis.

Beaumont, KFDM-TV, David Lowell

At the very least, get yourself a job at the campus radio station and read news on the air as much as they'll let you. Listen to the network anchors and top reporters. Don't try to copy them, but listen for what they share in common.

Corpus Christi, TV

Some surveys show that voice may be the single most important aspect of viewer preference when it comes to anchor preference.

Dallas, KDFW–TV, Jim Valentine

Slow down—take your time to pause after each "thought group" of words in a sentence, so the listener can absorb and "feel" what you are saying.

Houston, KIKK AM–FM, Chuck Wolf

Some of the best advice I've ever received in this business came from long-time KPRC News Director Ray Miller: "Write like people talk. Talk like you talk." I like to hear genuine enthusiasm and energy in a broadcaster's voice. Every word should convey "This is interesting!" to the listener. Too many people try to lower their voice pitch and end up with a loud monotone. One of the more difficult tasks I've encountered in this profession is that of instilling confidence in basic voice quality so that people can then learn to use what they have to best effect.

Houston, KPRC, Doug Ross

A voice is the most visible tool of our trade. If you do not develop the best voice possible you are trying to do the job without the proper tools. It's like trying to do surgery with a penknife.

Odessa, KOSA–TV, Don Scott

We put anchors in a formal setting and ask them to be "natural" . . . this also means their voice and this is tough to do. What I look for and encourage is the anchor and/or reporter to be themselves.The more natural and conversational they sound, the better. So many reporters have a lot of spark, then when the lights and camera go on, they become monotone, almost flat. Strive to have them put that spark in their delivery when the lights go on . . . strive for a "talking" tone.

Wichita Falls, KFDX-TV, Cindy L. Bradford

VIRGINIA

Voice is probably the #1 criterion used in hiring. When News Directors punch the eject button 15 seconds into an applicant's tape, they do it because that applicant sounds like an amateur, not a professional. Yet, sadly, far too many broadcast journalism programs ignore vocal training and few other resources are available. Probably 90% of our daily communications are verbal throughout our lives, yet no one really teaches us the correct way to speak. We breathe the wrong way, we develop bad habits, and many of us never shake them or learn better.

It's simple. If you're going to make your living with your voice, you should learn to use your voice effectively. It is as basic as learning how to type, and for a broadcaster it is just as important.

Charlottesville, WVIR-TV, David Cupp

Radio newscasters will, in their careers, be asked to deliver news in a variety of different styles. Anchors must be flexible.

I always like to work with people who have had musical training. Then, you can coach using terms like "accent," "staccato," "legato"—and be talking in terms you both understand.

In broadcast, either in news or in commercial production work, your voice is your instrument and your delivery must be "musical" to be both credible and understood.

Norfolk, WTAR–WLTY, Georgeann Herbert

While newspapers and television can use pictures to supplement their news coverage, in radio, voices are all we have. That's why it's particularly important for job applicants to have at least practiced their delivery on a tape recorder and listened to network newscasters for an idea of how news is presented. Newscasters should retain their individual style of delivery, while understanding communication is the main goal. Anything that interferes with effective communication on the radio will stand in the way of a successful career.

Richmond, Virginia News Network, Randy Davis

Use a talent coach at least 3–4 times per year, particularly just before a rating book.

Richmond, TV

Relax and talk to viewers not at them.

Roanoke, TV

WASHINGTON

Practice on being natural!

Seattle, KING–TV, Donald Varyu

Some on-air talent fail to grasp the meaning of the story they are reading and without that understanding they are unable to convey the meaning to their viewers. To be a good reader, the talent must first understand, and be knowledgeable of his copy. Knowing when to inflect your voice is also vital.

Yakima, KIMA–TV, T.J. Close

The voice isn't likely to make a reporter's career, but it could break it—or keep it from starting.

The proper use of voice is more important than any other element of a person's delivery.

Yakima, KNDO/KNDU, Roger Gadley

WEST VIRGINIA

The days of the stiff, robotic-like delivery seem to have left us and now the reporter who can communicate in an authoritative yet conversational manner will be the most effective. It is accepted by the viewer as if it is coming from a person rather than just a reporter.

Huntington, WSAZ–TV, William S. Cummings

In most cases, good voice broadcast quality can be obtained with practice. Early and constant work will help anyone willing to practice, even after a few years in broadcasting.

Oak Hill, WOAY–TV, Mike Jackson

WISCONSIN

Seek to find training in breathing and presentation. Get a double major in speech or drama. Learn your craft in radio or live public speaking. Continue to practice, practice. Don't just read when it's time to read, record and read aloud everything. Be open to critique.

Green Bay, WLUK–TV, Michael R. Gaede

Gone are the days of the stereotypical radio voice: the booming voice which caused us radio-types to proclaim "what pipes!" I look for an unusual voice quality, one which contributes to style!

Madison, WTDY/WMGN, Toni Denison

Practice makes perfect! And breaking old habits may be made easier through exercises!

Milwaukee, WVTV, Liz Talbot

Pronunciation Tests and Word Lists

The broadcast copy that follows may not be the most interesting material you have read or the best broadcast writing. What is significant about these stories, however, is that each one includes all forty of the phonemes of our language.

Tape record these stories and listen to them critically. Ask others such as your teacher, voice coach, or news director to listen to them. You may find that you are mispronouncing certain phonemes or dropping sounds. These stories will help you analyze your pronunciations and isolate particular phonemes that cause you difficulty. Once you have found your problem phonemes, consult the practice word lists that follow.

News Copy—Phoneme Tests

#1   If you are not planning to travel
      this weekend, you might want to
      plan a trip to the county fair. It
      begins tomorrow and continues until
      the twentieth. They put up the
      tents last night and will pull them
      down when it ends. You can try your
      hand at knocking over bottles,
      running races, popping balloons,
      and testing your strength in the
      lifting contest. Real animals will
      provide action as usual on Friday
      night as well as Sunday in the large
      arena. Officials thought boys and
      girls ought to be able to attend for
      under a dollar. Now that is the
      case. Admission is twenty-five
      cents for children and one dollar
      for adults. Lunch is available at
      the fairgrounds.

#2   Returns are trickling in from
      yesterday's primary election. The
      results were delayed due to a
      faulty computer in the Richmond
      Center. Democrat Hinton Royal is
      ranked first to overcome union
      official, Jim Sheffield, for
      council president. Controversial
      candidate, lawyer Roy Pool, put his
      position in jeopardy with awful
      standings in his own county. He was
      chosen by three delegates to start
      ahead, but he has yet to win. Pool
      needs just nine counties to get a
      victory.

Practice Word Lists

If you found that certain phonemes are difficult for you to pronounce correctly, the following word lists will help you practice the phonemes in words until you hear an improvement. The lists are arranged by vowel and consonant phonemes.

Vowels

/i/ bee

plea	seen	relief
eager	creep	achieve
beet	free	week
feel	key	illegal
easel	tease	intrigue
keep	sneeze	conceive

/ɪ/ bit

trip	hit	city
pit	fit	pity
wit	mitt	pretty
lick	drip	his
grin	thin	rib
skin	wrist	visit

/e/ say

race	lame	tame
case	way	waste
ace	rage	awake
pay	state	trait
lace	date	dismay
fray	make	neigh

/ε/ **bet**

head	check	pest
debt	step	red
left	edit	exit
kept	men	theft
get	thread	deaf
wreck	guess	ten

/æ/ **at**

sat	pat	lamb
cap	sand	plan
gap	hack	trap
match	laugh	plant
jam	than	answer
last	mad	parrot

/ɑ/ **spa**

calm	odd	argue
car	harsh	bark
smart	shark	father
palm	cargo	heart
arbor	armor	Hawaii
parked	dark	charm

/ɔ/ **caw**

awful	lost	gnaw
clause	coffin	hall
fought	dog	sought
law	wall	auto
mall	August	thought
yawn	pawn	straw

/o/ oak

own	soak	pillow
cone	tore	explore
bone	omit	both
zone	dough	willow
clove	toe	oration
beau	hotel	cooperate

/u/ two

you	who	school
food	crude	tattoo
June	gloom	spoon
two	grew	moon
shoot	ooze	rule
blue	screw	drool

/U/ put

wool	poor	roof
full	look	nook
should	shook	wood
bush	bull	crook
book	stood	brook
tour	cook	push

/ə/ above

alone	cut	money
summer	brother	jump
rug	love	circus
truck	luck	lion
run	hut	spud
done	plum	sofa

/ɚ/ **father**

amber	alter	dirt
deserve	otter	squirm
return	ponder	rehearse
worth	favor	jerk
verb	mirror	disturb
skirt	birth	confirm

Diphthongs

/ju/ **use**

union	funeral	humiliate
mute	uniform	music
pupil	puberty	numerous
view	bugle	fabulous
human	amuse	tabulate
eulogy	refusal	unify

/aɪ/ **eye**

sky	alive	strike
fire	iodine	light
time	nice	pantomime
reply	fight	China
deny	whine	biceps
bias	rhyme	bright

/aʊ/ **cow**

mouse	cloud	how
powder	ouch	devour
allowance	loud	blouse

couch	scowl	South
foul	sour	impound
anyhow	found	endow

/ɔɪ/ toy

hoist	doily	oily
annoy	avoid	exploit
loiter	Joyce	loyal
boy	voice	toil
joy	tabloid	spoil
coil	coy	choice

Consonants

/t/ to (Voiceless)

Initial	Medial	Final
tea	attend	light
tool	Utah	suit
talk	rotate	elite
tube	intend	sweet
turn	utensil	missed
town	entire	laughed

/d/ do (Voiced)

Initial	Medial	Final
den	ladder	dad
dime	handle	told
dole	underneath	yield
dollar	ending	ride
dame	condition	bird
dip	idea	gold

/p/ pop (Voiceless)

Initial	Medial	Final
pay	reaper	keep
peg	clapped	mope
poem	carpet	hoop
poke	wrapper	weep
powder	sweeping	asleep
position	typify	pipe

/b/ boy (Voiced)

Initial	Medial	Final
bay	saber	lab
bait	flabby	web
bottom	baby	probe
bike	ebony	lobe
base	habit	curb
band	obey	bib

/k/ key (Voiceless)

Initial	Medial	Final
curl	packing	risk
kitten	echo	ask
cash	kicked	caulk
keep	chicken	fork
come	wicked	slick
quit	rocky	dike

/g/ got (Voiced)

Initial	Medial	Final
gear	haggle	bug
guest	toggle	vogue

gossip	figure	plug
gift	disguise	league
gallon	tiger	drug
ghost	embargo	jog

/f/ fit (Voiceless)

Initial	Medial	Final
face	raffle	calf
fail	define	life
flour	reference	half
fun	infest	enough
fence	safer	golf
physics	coffee	chef

/v/ van (Voiced)

Initial	Medial	Final
veal	paved	love
vein	ravel	prove
vapor	avid	forgive
victory	driver	revolve
vowel	seven	dove
vice	heaven	have

/θ/ thin (Voiceless)

Initial	Medial	Final
thank	method	myth
thrill	Catholic	wrath
thick	birthday	cloth
thigh	pathos	mouth
theme	esthetic	path
thaw	nothing	faith

/ð/ them (Voiced)

Initial	Medial	Final
this	mother	teethe
though	breathing	smooth
that	feather	soothe
then	clothing	blithe
there	northern	clothe
the	heathen	bathe

/s/ say (Voiceless)

Initial	Medial	Final
such	asset	bless
steak	insert	peace
stay	essay	mouse
spill	tracing	kiss
skid	bossy	nervous
space	history	purpose

/z/ zip (Voiced)

Initial	Medial	Final
zebra	spasm	ease
zenith	music	lads
Xerox	desire	wise
zephyr	reason	rhymes
zoom	resign	symbols
zircon	used	browse

/ʃ/ she (Voiceless)

Initial	Medial	Final
shall	anxious	fresh
ship	direction	mustache
shy	fashion	wish

sugar	special	cash
chic	tissue	leash
shoe	washer	fresh

/ʒ/ casual (Voiced)

Initial	Medial	Final
/ʒ/ does not	vision	beige
occur as an	pleasure	camouflage
initial sound	occasion	garage
in English	usual	rouge
except in a	persuasion	mirage
few words	Asia	corsage
borrowed		
from French		
(e.g., genre).		

/h/ hit (Voiceless)

Initial	Medial	Final
hand	behave	/h/ does
human	perhaps	not occur in
hotel	somehow	the final
humid	inherit	position.
whose	overhaul	
heart	apprehend	

/tʃ/ chip (Voiceless)

Initial	Medial	Final
chafe	teacher	much
charge	lecture	catch
chastise	bachelor	reach
chicken	question	lunch
challenge	picture	search
chalk	fracture	coach

/dʒ/ Jim (Voiced)

Initial	Medial	Final
jaw	adjacent	age
joke	education	badge
just	collegiate	rage
genius	courageous	cage
judge	danger	college
jar	soldier	edge

/w/ was (Voiced or Voiceless)

Initial	Medial	Final
wear	question	/w/ occurs
wet	forward	only preced-
witch	quarter	ing a vowel
witness	somewhere	sound.
water	quack	
word	quit	

/j/ yet (Voiced)

Initial	Medial	Final
yes	lawyer	/j/ occurs
yellow	champion	only preced-
youth	pavilion	ing a vowel
yearling	genius	sound.
yeast	million	
year	civilian	

/r/ run (Voiced)

Initial	Medial	Final
read	error	bar
wreck	erode	ignore

wrap	moron	mare
roof	bury	tour
wrote	tarot	chair
realize	purely	appear

/l/ love (Voiced)

Initial	Medial	Final
lip	follow	zeal
letter	elope	apple
lawn	believe	pearl
late	palace	kale
lake	blind	style
lean	tilt	foil

/m/ miss (Voiced)

Initial	Medial	Final
may	remove	beam
murder	hammer	dime
mail	emblem	autumn
mock	emanate	bomb
middle	remind	custom
murky	climbing	theme

/n/ now (Voiced)

Initial	Medial	Final
not	plaintive	bean
gnaw	dawning	spoon
pneumatic	sentence	done
know	pants	brown
nation	respond	began
knife	telephoned	loosen

/ŋ/ sing (Voiced)

Initial	Medial	Final
/ŋ/ does not	length	throng
occur in	kingly	belong
the initial	wrongly	among
position.	gangster	thing
	ink	sprang
	youngster	stung

Relaxation and Warm-Up Routines

This routine can be done anytime you feel the need to relax before on-air work. The goal is to fully relax the body with special emphasis on relaxing the throat area.

1) Stand in a relaxed manner—shoulders relaxed, knees slightly bent.

2) Take 2 abdominal-diaphragmatic breaths. Abdomen goes out as you inhale and comes in as you exhale. (If difficulty is encountered, complete the breath and try again until 2 relaxed abdominal-diaphragmatic breaths are accomplished—avoid tensing when an error is made.)

3) Neck relaxers—very slowly drop your chin to your chest then roll your head up to your right shoulder. Roll your head back down to your chest then roll your head up to your left shoulder. Bring your chin back down to your chest. Repeat slowly 3 times. (Do not roll your head back. This may cause neck injuries.)

Neck Turns—Look straight ahead. Rotate the head slowly and look over each shoulder twice as if you were signalling an exaggerated "no."

4) Pull your shoulders up toward the ears. Tense and hold. Drop your shoulders and relax. Do this exercise twice.

5) Breathing exercises—Take 2 abdominal-diaphragmatic breaths followed by 1 complete breath. For complete breath, inhale/exhale to the count of:

> 3—with abdominal-diaphragm muscles
> 3—with chest muscles
> 1—clavicular
> hold for 2 seconds and exhale, bringing shoulders down, chest in, and abdomen in.

Take 1 abdominal-diaphragmatic breath and exhale an /ɑ/ ("ah") with the mouth fully open and relaxed. Make the sound forceful and steady. Concentrate on placement of the sound behind the front teeth and control of exhalation.

6) Check for tension—if you are not relaxed, repeat the series.

Broadcast Voice
Warm-Ups

This collection of warm-ups is taken from the preceding chapters. They are arranged here so that you can select the ones that are most effective for you and make them part of your daily routine. You might want to put some of these on notecards to carry with you or post in your sound booth. Try doing warm-ups as you are driving to work and several times throughout the day.

All professional athletes and performers know that warm-ups are important. Do not be embarrassed doing these vocal warm-ups prior to your on-air work. Integrating warm-ups into your daily routine shows your professionalism.

1) With one hand on your abdominal area, take a deep inhalation, pushing your hand out. Sustain any of the following vowel sounds on exhalation:

- /ɑ/ ("ah") as in spa
- /ɔ/ ("aw") as in caw
- /u/ ("u") as in two

Time each vowel production. Stop vocalization when the sound begins to waver or sound weak. At first, your times may be in the ten to fifteen second range. Try to build your control of exhalation by adding a few seconds each time until you can sustain a vowel for twenty to thirty seconds. Keep a record of your progress.

2) Grasp your body so that your fingers touch in the front of your abdominal area and your thumbs reach around toward your back. Take a deep inhalation that pushes your fingers apart. With that breath, vocalize any of the following lists. Make certain that you do not take in any additional small gulps of air. You should be measuring your breath support by exhaling only one inhalation. Keep a record of how far you go each time.

- Repeat the days of the week.
- Count by ones or tens.
- Repeat the months of the year.
- Say the alphabet.

3) This exercise is called the "Countdown to Calm Down." If you practice this enough, it will relieve some of the tension that precedes each taping. Establish a habit of using it in the sound booth or for stand-ups. It will break the tension of the day and get you ready to record.

Take a deep abdominal-diaphragmatic inhalation and say, "Broadcast Voice Handbook story, take one." (You would replace this title with your story slug as you make this part of your routine when you begin recording.) Now inhale deeply again, and say, "Three, two, one." Inhale a third time and begin your story. For a practice story opener you can say, "Broadcasters are finding that a few simple breathing exercises can make a difference."

(This method of beginning your taping may seem too slow or time-consuming at first. I have found with clients, however, that the four or five seconds needed for the additional breathing are well worth it. Many clients report that they do fewer takes of each piece with this method. They often are pleased with their voice in the first reading after using their countdown time to calm down.)

4) Take a deep abdominal-diaphragmatic inhalation and say, "Good evening, I'm (your name) and this is Eyewitness News." Exhale any remaining air. Inhale again and say the phrase twice. Continue building the number of times you can repeat the phrase on one inhalation maintaining an appropriate pitch and volume. Keep a record of your progress.

5) Yawning has been used for centuries as a technique to relax the throat. A good yawn relaxes the larynx and throat and brings in a good air supply. Practice yawning for relaxation. Drop the jaw and think of what a good yawn feels like. Yawning is sometimes contagious, so take the opportunity to yawn when you see others doing so. Add a sigh at the end of your yawn to feel your relaxed, open throat. After yawning, say this phrase with the same open throat, "How many hats does Henry have?" Say this several times, trying to preserve the open feeling.

Most of us tend to hold tension in our shoulders, upper back, and neck. To relieve this tension try these warm-ups. Be careful not to stretch your muscles too much.

6) Clasp your hands behind your back. Squeeze your shoulder blades together and raise your arms slightly, tilting your head back. Hold your arms up at the point you feel resistance. Release. Repeat this warm-up until your shoulders and upper back feel relaxed.

7) Place your hands on your shoulders. Rotate your shoulders by bringing your elbows together in front, moving them down, back, and up in a circular movement. Continue five times in one direction and five times in the opposite direction.

8) Neck relaxers—very slowly drop your chin to your chest and roll your head up to your right shoulder. Roll your head back down to your chest and roll your head up to your left shoulder. Bring your chin back down to your chest. Repeat slowly three times. (Do not roll your head back. This may cause neck injuries.)

9) Neck Turns—Look straight ahead. Rotate your head slowly and look over each shoulder twice as if you were signalling an exaggerated "no."

10) To relax the throat, take a deep abdominal-diaphragmatic breath and exhale an /ɑ/ ("ah") sound. Inhale again and exhale an /u/ ("ou") sound as in "you." Inhale a third time and exhale an "m" sound. Feel the resonance in the nasal cavity for the "m."

11) To gain flexibility in pitch, say "one" at your normal pitch level. Now go up one step in pitch and say "two." Go up another step in pitch and say "three."Go back down to your normal pitch with "three, two, one." Now go down in pitch one step and say "two." Go down another step and say "three." Go back up to your normal pitch. This process would look like this:

```
        three three
    two             two
one                       one one                        one
                              two             two
                          three three
```

You might want to trace the steps in pitch in the air with your finger as your voice produces them. Tape recording this warm-up work will help you hear if you are really producing the pitch changes you hope for.

12) Continue pitch work by saying the phrase:

```
                    up
"My voice is going       in pitch."
"My voice is going       in pitch."
                  down
```

Repeat these two phrases until you feel comfortable with your pitch changes.

13) Use this phrase to expand your pitch range:

```
                               up."
                          up
                       up
                     up
                   up
"I can make my voice go

"I can make my voice go
                      down
                          down
                             down
                                down
                                   down."
```

When doing this warm-up do not push your voice into an artificially high or low pitch. Going too high or low can cause vocal fatigue and possible abuse. For a falsetto, for example, the vocal folds are pulled excessively tight, and they lose their wave-like motion. As with any unnatural position of the folds, this can be harmful.

14) Sing up the musical scale by singing:

```
                    do
                  ti
                 la
               sol
             fa
           mi
         re
       do
```

Repeat this until you feel comfortable with these eight tones.

15) To improve placement and increase oral resonance, bend forward from the waist at a ninety degree angle. Keep your neck straight so you are looking down at the floor. Flex your knees slightly to prevent strain on your back. (If you have a bad back, do this Warm-Up on all fours with your back straight and your face parallel to the floor.) Repeat this phrase, aiming the sound at the floor as you look down:

- Good evening, this is (your name) reporting for Eyewitness News.

Feel the sound resonating in your oral cavity before the sound falls toward the floor. Concentrate on hitting the floor with the sound. Now straighten up and repeat the phrase trying to keep the placement the same.

16) The sound /ɑ/ ("ah") opens the mouth the widest and lowers the tongue. Doctors use this to look at our throats, and you can use it to increase resonance. Say the following words, preceded by "ah" and try to maintain the wide opening:

ah	far
ah	father
ah	got
ah	factor
ah	back
ah	tackle
ah	awesome
ah	awful
ah	law
ah	go
ah	own
ah	gold

17) The word "awe" puts your lips and cheeks in a position to have the best oral resonance. This position is the reverse

of a smile, which pulls the lips back and tenses the cheeks. Say the word "awe" before each number as you count from one to ten to feel the relaxed, forward position of the cheeks and lips.

- Awe—1, awe—2, awe—3, etc.

18) To increase jaw openness for better resonance, place your chin between your thumb and index finger. Repeat these words feeling the jaw drop as much as possible:

- back, back, back, back
- sack, sack, sack, sack
- bad, bad, bad, bad
- yard, yard, yard, yard
- am, am, am, am
- accent, accent, accent, accent
- sang, sang, sang, sang

19) It is important to continue to work on placement of the sound waves behind the front teeth. Decide what imagery you want to use to see the sound beginning at the diaphragm and moving up from the lungs through the vocal folds and into the pharynx. Watch the sound waves making the important ninety degree turn to enter the oral cavity and see the sound waves hitting the back of the front teeth or the cup above the alveolar ridge before leaving the mouth. You might think of a beam of light, a hose, a tube, or anything that helps you visualize this path. Now repeat these vowel sounds with your eyes closed and your concentration on the sound waves making their journey:

- /ɑ/ "ah," /ɔ/ "awe," /i/ "eee"
- ah, awe, eee
- ah, awe, eee

Next, say this sentence, concentrating on the same image:

- My voice begins at the diaphragm, is pushed from the lungs, passes through the vocal folds into the pharynx, and turns to resonate in my oral cavity.

Keep working with this phrase until you can say it with one exhalation and imagine it moving through the vocal mechanism.

20) Say these phonemes, exaggerating the mouth positions:

- /ɑ/ as in spa
- /ɔ/ as in caw
- /u/ as in two
- /i/ as in bee

Open the mouth wide for /ɑ/, round the lips for /ɔ/, pull the lips forward in a pucker for the /u/ phoneme, and smile widely for /i/. Continue to say these phonemes in an exaggerated manner, gliding from one to the next. Use this series of phonemes as a warm-up before going on air. After repeating them a dozen times or more in an exaggerated manner you should feel your mouth becoming more flexible.

21) Continuing with the exaggerated stretching found in the last Warm-Up, repeat this sentence extending the vowel phonemes:

- You see Oz.

Pucker the lips tightly for the /u/ in "you." Pull the lips back in a wide smile for the /i/ in "see," and drop the jaw and open wide for the /ɑ/ in "Oz." Repeat this sentence with these exaggerated lip positions as many times as you need to in order to warm up your articulators.

22) Repeat the following sentences as fast as you can while preserving the consonant plosive formations:

- Put a cup. Put a cup. Put a cup. Put a cup.

- Drink buttermilk. Drink buttermilk. Drink buttermilk.

Rapid repetition of these sentences will help warm up your tongue. Say these sentences rapidly before on-air work.

       23) Chewing and talking at the same time has been used extensively to improve articulation because chewing loosens the jaw and tongue. To practice this, pretend you have just taken a big bite from an apple and count out loud while you chew. You can also say the months of the year, days of the week, or the alphabet for this Warm-Up. You should exaggerate your chewing while you speak.

Practice Broadcast Copy

The broadcast copy given in this Appendix has been gathered for your convenience to provide practice material.

Susanne Fowler, Assistant Managing Editor-Broadcast for United Press International, provided the copy that follows. She explains UPI's philosophy and broadcast writing techniques:

The UPI National Newswire copy supplied for this book represents several hours of national and international news, sports, financial, weather, and features information. You see the stories as they appeared on the broadcast wire February 12, 1990.

United Press International pioneered writing for the ear in the 1930s and continues the tradition today at its National Broadcast headquarters in Chicago.

We cover the news around the world, around the clock.

The broadcast wire is designed to be a timely, air-ready product for those who need it to be and to provide packaged breaking and background material for larger newsrooms to mesh with their own video and audio tape.

As you know, broadcast writing is special. It is somewhere in between scholarly prose and street slang. It takes professionals to write it and professionals to read it.

As Fowler points out, the stories that follow came right off the wire. You can read the stories as they appear, or you may want to experiment with rewriting certain stories before you mark them for practice. Most newsrooms develop their own style of writing and do not use wire stories as they appear here. They rewrite or edit the stories to reflect the style of their newsroom.

WORLD HEADLINES

-O-(
After more than 27 years behind bars for political crimes, South African black nationalist Nelson Mandela (Mahn-DEH'-lah) will be freed today (at 8:00 a-m e-s-t). In honor of the occassion, the white minority government released the first official photograph of 71-year-old Mandela since 1966. (
(
As media sources throughout the world interrupted regular programming to carry President F-W de Klerk's announcement of Mandela's impending release, South African T-V viewers were watching a live cricket match. (
-O-(
Secretary of State Baker says his grilling yesterday by senior Soviet government officials during his historic appearance before a parliamentary committee in Moscow reflects the new, more honest U-S-Soviet relationship. (
-O-(
James ''Buster'' Douglas connected with a left uppercut and sent heavyweight champ Mike Tyson sprawling through the 10th round of tonight's heavyweight title match in Tokyo. The knockout blow sets Douglas atop the heavyweight boxing world. (
-O-(
Military sources say Thai (Tigh) border forces killed eight Burmese soldiers who had crossed the frontier into Thailand earlier today while preparing to attack a guerrilla camp inside Burma. The Thai forces attacked when the Burmese personnel ignored warning shots. (
-O-(
Celebrations in South Africa over word that black nationalist leader Nelson Mandela will be released from prison today have left eight people dead. Police reportedly fired to break up mobs of blacks hurling stones and petrol bombs. (
-O-(
Authorities in New Mexico are searching for two gunmen who left seven people shot... four fatally... in a Las Cruces (KROO'-says) bowling alley. Police say three of the dead were a father and his two young daughters. (
-O-(
NASA engineers believe they have fixed the computer glitch aboard the Galileo Jupiter probe that caused the robot's primary camera to malfunction. The probe had just completed an otherwise flawless flyby of Venus. (
-O-(
Soviet Prime Minister Ryzhkov (RIGHZH'-kawf) is in Thailand today on an official two-day visit. Talks with Thai leaders are expected to focus on the Cambodian conflict and expansion of Soviet economic ties with the region. (
-O-(
A published report (in the Miami Herald) says drug traffickers in Miami have laundered hundreds of Millions of dollars in cocaine profits through several city institutions. (
(
A six-month investigation (by the Herald) found that Miami leads the nation with a more than five-BILLION-dollar cash surplus in its banking system, a tell-tale sign of the drug trade. (
(

-0-<
South African police set up road blocks around the prison facility
from which former African national Congress leader Nelson Mandela
(Mahn-DEH'-lah) will emerge today a free man. Mandela has been jailed
more than 27 years. <
-0-<
Authorities outside Seattle say they're NOT sure if the human
skeletal remains discovered yesterday are another victim of the
unidentified ``Green River Killer.'' The serial killer is blamed for the
deaths of 41 women. <
-0-<
Soviet Prime Minister Ryzhkov (RIGHZH'-kawf) is in Thailand for two
days of talks aimed at getting Cambodian peace talks on track. Although
the Thai (Tigh) and Soviet governments support opposite sides, they are
urging peace. <
-0-<
West Coast environmentalists dispute a Mexican claim that oil
spills along the Pacific shoreline have hindered gray whales from their
annual migration to the warm waters of Baja (BAH'-hah), Mexico. <
-0-<
After more than 27 years in prison... black South African
nationalist Nelson Mandela (Man-DEH'-lah) will go free today. Police
have set up road blocks around the Cape Town prison from which Mandela
will be released. <
<
Following his release, Mandela, who is 71... will be driven into
Cape Town for a news conference and rally in the heart of the city.
President de Klerk announced the release yesterday to set up talks with
the black opposition. <
-0-<
Secretary of State Baker is in Romania today on the final leg of a
six-day Eastern Europe visit. During his trip, Baker spoke with Soviet
legislators as well as government and opposition leaders in Romania and
Bulgaria. <
-0-<
Two New York policeman answering to a nine-one-one call from a
subway station last night found a 10-months pregnant woman unable to
wait another moment. The officers delivered a healthy baby boy to
18-year-old Sydell Golthin. <
-0-<
New Mexico police are searching for two gunmen who rounded up seven
people in a bowling alley yesterday... shot them and set a fire in an
apparent robbery. four of the seven victims were killed in the shooting.
-0-<
The Coast Guard in Southern California says the a
394-thousand-gallon spill of Huntington Beach has spoiled 13 miles of
shoreline in the last four days. The spill resulted from the tanker
apparently being pierced by its own anchor. <
-0-<
Eight anti-abortion protesters jailed indefinitely in Portland,
Oregon, for civil contempt have decided to remain in prison rather than
pledge 10-thousand dollars each in assets as a condition of release. <
-0-<
A published report in New York (in the Daily News) says Ivana Trump
is dumping her BILLIONAIRE husband Donald Trump because he betrayed her.
The story quotes unnamed sources which Mrs. Trump would neither confirm
or deny. <

In Zambia, the African National Congress says it welcomes today's
release of its leader, Nelson Mandela (Man-DEH'-lah), from a South
African prison. However, it doubted whether Pretoria would meet all its
conditions for power-sharing talks. <
-0-<

Secretary of State Baker has wrapped up his Eastern European tour after visiting Romania today on the final leg of a weeklong visit to Eastern Europe. Baker spent the night in Bulgaria, where he told leaders that Washington doubts the sincerity of their proposed reforms. (
    -0- (
Philippine President Aquino (Ah-KEE'-noh) intends to ask Washington about shortfalls in U-S aid used to pay for the use of two strategic military bases. Aquino says she has NO plans to meet Defense Secretary Cheney, who will be in Manila next week. (
    -0- (
West German Chancellor Kohl left Moscow today after a one-day day trip. Kohl says Soviet President Gorbachev (GOHRB'-ah-chawf) promised to leave the time frame for German reunification for Germans to decide. (
    -0- (
The Soviet news agency Tass says two Soviet cosmonauts blasted off today for a rendezvous with the orbiting Mir (Meer) space station. The new pair will replace two other cosmonauts who have spent six months in the giant orbiting complex. (
    -0- (
Despite his 10th-round knockout of heavyweight champ Mike Tyson... James ''Buster'' Douglas isn't wearing the champ's belts yet. Douglas K-O'd Tyson in the 10th round of their 12-round title bout today in Tokyo. (
(
But the World Boxing Council and the World Boxing Association are declaring the world heavyweight championship vacant pending a review of Tyson's controversial eighth-round knockdown of Douglas. (
    -0- (
Nelson Mandela (Man-DEH'-lah) walked to freedom today after being driven to the gates of Victor Verster Prison in Paarl, South Africa. The 71-year-old black nationalist leader was greeted by chanting and cheering crowds waving African National Congress flags. (
(
The silver-haired Mandela headed into Cape Town after his release, where a new conference and rally is scheduled. Mandela's unconditional release from a life prison sentence was announced by the white-minority government yesterday. (
    -0- (
An adviser to Mikhail Gorbachev (MEEK'-high-yehl GOHRB'-ah-chawf) says the Soviet leader will NOT oppose German reunification. But the adviser adds the Kremlin does NOT want its troops removed from East Germany if U-S troops remain on West German soil. (
    -0- (
Secretary of State Baker is on his way to Ireland, where he'll make a brief stop before beginning the journey home. Baker held talks earlier in the day with Romanian leaders as he wrapped up a six-day Eastern European tour. (
    -0- (
Mike Tyson says in his heart, he's still the champ. But in reality, the status of Tyson's International Boxing Federation belt is unclear after a knockout last night in Tokyo. But James Douglas' apparent victory is being reviewed. (

    -0- (
A new chapter opened in South Africa's political history today as black nationalist Nelson Mandela walked out of Victor Verster prison a free man. Mandela's release comes 27 years after he was sentenced to life for sabotage. (
(
The 71-year-old African National Congress leader was driven to the prison gate in a car and then walked to freedom hand-in-hand with his wife, Winnie. There was NO immediate explanation for a more than 45 minute-delay in Mandela's release. (

-o-<
Secretary of State Baker headed to Shannon, Ireland, today after wrapping up a six-day tour of Eastern Europe. Baker earlier held four hours of talks with Romanian leaders in Bucharest, where the government sought to allay U-S concerns over its commitment to democratic reform. <
-o-<
Officials reports from Tehran say massive crowds marched through the streets of Iran's capital today, chanting slogans and carrying huge pictures of the late Ayatollah Khomeini as the country marked the 11th anniversary of its revolution. <
-o-<
The Soviet Union sent two cosmonauts into space today for the Mir (meer) space station where they will replace two other cosmonauts who have spent six months in the giant orbiting complex. <
-o-<
Secretary of State Baker promised Romania 80-Million dollars in humanitarian food aid today while wrapping up a six-day tour of Eastern Europe. But Baker linked any further U-S economic assistance to Romania to free elections and moves toward a free-market economy. <
<
Baker is now on his way to Ottawa, Canada, where he'll join a NATO-Warsaw Pact conference. The meeting is to discuss the establishment of an ''open skies'' military inspection plan covering 23 countries in Europe and North America. <
-o-<
The government of India today accused Pakistan of interfering in its internal affairs by supporting pro-secession Moslems in the troubled Indian province of Kashmir Valley. The government urged its neighbor to pursue a ''path of peace.'' <
-o-<
Illinois State Police have issued a nationwide alert for six prisoners who escaped from the Joliet Correctional Center by cutting through bars and a fence. They were discovered missing this morning. Police say three of the convicts are considered extremely dangerous. <
-o-<
Commentator Andy Rooney says in a syndicated column published today that he did NOT make the racist remarks attributed to him by a Los Angeles newspaper. Rooney was suspended for three months by C-B-S for allegedly making the offensive comments. <
-o-<
Trial gets underway tomorrow in Memphis for the only black congressman in Tennessee history. Representative Harold Ford was indicted in 1987 on 19 counts of bank fraud, mail fraud and conspiracy to defraud the government. <
-o-<
In Milton, Florida, opening statements will begin tomorrow in the murder trial of a spiritual adviser who allegedly persuaded a woman to starve her four-year-old daughter and beat her to exorcise demons. Mary Nicholson is charged in the 1988 starvation death of Kimberly McZinc. <
-o-<
Newly freed African National Congress leader Nelson Mandela told a news conference in Cape Town today that black South Africans have ''waited too long'' for freedom and must intensify the struggle on all fronts. <
<
Mandela called on white South Africans to join the march to freedom and said South Africa's racial conflict- quoting now- ''canNOT take place above the heads or behind the backs of our people.'' He said Pretoria's future can only be determined by voting in democratic elections on a non-racial basis. <
-o-<

Administration sources say President Bush and the leaders of three
Andean nations plan to sign ``a document of agreements'' at this week's
drug summit in Colombia. The sources say the document will commit the
leaders to an unprecedented war on drugs. (
   -0-(
Secretary of State Baker today wound up a weeklong trip to the
Soviet Union and Eastern Europe. During a visit to Bucharest, Baker
promised Romania 80-Million dollars in humanitarian food aid, but he
linked it to free elections. (
   -0-(
Illinois State Police are searching for six prisoners who broke out
of the Joliet Correctional Center. Police say three of the six are
considered extremely dangerous. The fugitives escaped by cutting through
bars and a fence. (
   -0-(
Nelson Mandela told South African blacks today they had NO option
but to continue an armed struggle against apartheid (uh-PAHR'-tayt). The
black nationalist spoke to some 100-thousand people in downtown Cape
Town, his first public appearance after 27 years in prison. (
   (
Within hours of his release from Victor Verster prison, Mandela
also offered an olive branch to whites, saying there is room in a free
South Africa for all races. He said he hopes freedom can be achieved
through negotiation. (
   -0-(
In Washington, Capitol Hill lawmakers appear UNwilling to call for
the immediate easing of sanctions against South Africa, despite
Mandela's release. A State Department official says the Bush
administration is reviewing its policy on South Africa. (
   -0-(
President Bush heads to Colombia this week for an anti-drug summit.
Administration sources say Bush and the leaders of Colombia, Peru and
Bolivia will sign a sweeping plan that will commit them to an
UNprecedented war on drugs. (
   -0-(
   (
(CAPE TOWN, South Africa)- Black nationalist leader Nelson Mandela
(Man-DEH'-lah) made his first public appearance today after 27 years in
prison. He was released earlier today, and was driven to Cape Town,
where he addressed a crowd estimated at more than 100-thousand. He told
the crowd the armed struggle against apartheid (uh-PAHR'-tayt) must
continue. But he offered an olive branch to whites, saying there's room
in a free South Africa for all races. Before he arrived at Cape Town,
violence erupted in the crowd that had gathered around the city hall.
Witnesses say police opened fire on parts of the crowd who were throwing
bottles and smashing storefront windows. Some reports say as many as 200
people were wounded, and an unconfirmed report says two people were
killed. (
   -0-(
Nelson Mandela (Man-DEH'-lah) is a free man today, released after
27 years of what he calls ``lonely'' imprisonment. The 71-year-old black
nationalist leader spoke to a crowd estimated at tens of thousands in
downtown Cape Town, South Africa. (
   (
As Mandela drove to the rally, police fired on people throwing
bottles and looting shops. The casualty count is unclear with one
unconfirmed radio report saying one black was fatally shot and another
was stabbed to death. (
   -0-(
A U-S official who helped prepare for this week's drug summit in
Colombia says a draft agreement has already been worked out. One
Democrat says the summit is- quoting New York Representative Charles
Rangel- ``better than invading countries.'' (

-o- (

Secretary of State Baker wound up a weeklong trip to the Soviet Union and Eastern Europe by flying to Bucharest today, where he met with Romanian leaders. Baker promised an immediate 80-Million dollars in food aid. (

-o- (

An imaging expert says he thinks Americans are in for ''a powerful statement.'' Cameras aboard NASA's Voyager-1 probe will take pictures Tuesday that'll provide an historic family portrait of the solar system's seven planets. (

-o- (

Government and civil rights leaders around the world are hailing Nelson Mandela's (uh-PAHR'-tayts) release today from a South African prison. In Atlanta, Martin Luther King's widow, Coretta Scott King, called it a ''bold step toward peacefully dismantling apartheid (Man-DEH'-lah).'' (

(

Mandela told a massive crowd in Cape Town that a peaceful settlement to ending apartheid (uh-PAHR'-tayt) is possible. But he says South Africa's white minority government has a long way to go toward reform before the black majority is ready to rest. (

-o- (

Lebanese security sources say rival Christian forces are preparing for further bloody confrontations by reinforcing their positions northeast of Beirut. The preparations coincide with daylong sporadic artillery and rocket exchanges between the warring sides in east Beirut. (

-o- (

A nationwide manhunt is on for two Hispanic men believed to be the gunmen in a weekend attack at a bowling alley in Las Cruces, Mexico, in which seven people were shot in an apparent attempt to eliminate witnesses to a robbery. Four of the victims died. (

-o- (

News reports (in the Washington Post) say Washington D-C Mayor Marion Barry was warned by his attorney NOT to trust anyone months before his arrest on cocaine charges. The reports say Barry was told to be cautious because he could be the target of an undercover sting operation. (

-o- (

South Carolina Republican Strom Thurmond will crisscross his state tomorrow while announcing his bid for a seventh term in the U-S Senate. The 87-year-old lawmaker says he's as fit as a man in his 50s. (

-o- (

The trial of fired Exxon Valdez (Val-DEEZ') skipper Joseph Hazelwood enters its third week tomorrow in Anchorage, Alaska, with the testimony of two Coast Guard radar watchers. Testimony last week largely focused on Hazelwood's drinking. (

-o- (

Authorities in Mansfield, Ohio, say today that twin brothers played out their dream of being law officers during a stand-off with police. The two held a sheriff hostage Friday before one fatally shot his sibling and then himself. (

-o- (

Perrier has found the culprit! The French mineral water company says an employee in the bottling plant defied company orders and use benzene to ''de-grease'' something... leading to small traces of benzene in U-S bound Perrier bottles. (

-11- (

The leader of West Germany's ultra-right wing Republican party has founded an East German affiliate party. About 100 mostly-youthful East Germans gathered in West Berlin today for the founding of the party. (

-11- (

Polish Prime Minister Mazowiecki (Mah-zoh-VYEHT'-skee) told 300
Solidarity trade union delegates in Gdansk (Guh-DAHNSK') today that the
government needs their support as it pushes on with its harsh austerity
program. <
    -11-<
Indian soldiers opened fire on a crowd of Pakistanis that charged
across the border today... killing at least two and wounding six more.
The Pakistanis were shouting anti-Indian slogans as they charged across
the disputed border in the Kashmir region. <
<
The Indian government is warning the Pakistani government that it's
meddling in Indian affairs by supporting Moslem separatists in Kashmir.
Both countries claim the Moslem province as their own. The Moslem
residents want to be part of Pakistan. <

WORLD BRIEFS

    -11-<
South African authorities erected roadblocks around the prison
facility from which black nationalist leader Nelson Mandela
(Mahn-DEH'-lah) will be freed later today (at 8 a-m e-s-t). Nearly
two-thousand white extremists greeted yesterday's word of Mandela's
release after more than 27 years of imprisonment by marching through
Pretoria and chanting for his death. <
    -11-<
Authorities near Seattle say it's too early to comment if human
skeletal remains unearthed in a wooded area yesterday are those of
another victim of the so-called ''Green River Killer.'' The unknown
killer has been blamed for the slayings of 41 women and linked to the
disappearance of eight others in the Pacific Northwest. Officials think
the grisly string of murders ended in 1984. <
    -11-<
Soviet Prime Minister Ryzhkov (RIGHZH'-kawf) arrived today in
Thailand to kick off a two-day state visit observers believe will focus
on regional peace as well as an expansion of Soviet economic ties with
Thailand. While the Soviets and Thais (Tighz) provide weapons to
opposite sides in the Cambodian conflict, each government has urged its
Cambodian allies to find a political solution to the bloodshed. <
    -11-<
A San Francisco NON-profit group denies a Mexican report that says
oil spills along the Pacific coast have severely limited the annual
migration of gray whales from Alaska to their breeding grounds in Baja
(BAH'-hah), Mexico. A spokeswoman for Oceanic Society Expeditions says
whale observers and environmentalists tell her this year's migration of
the giant mammals is NO different than previous years. <
    -11-<
A published report in New York (in The Daily News) quotes unnamed
sources saying BILLIONAIRE Donald Trump is being dumped by his
Czechoslovakian-born wife of 12 years. Ivana Trump reportedly told the
sources she was ending the marriage because- quoting the sources-
''Donald was betraying her.'' Mr. Trump could NOT be reached for
comment. Mrs. Trump declined to confirm the story. <
    -11-<
Halfway into the 10th round of last night's scheduled 12-round
heavyweight title fight in Tokyo, James ''Buster'' Douglas crunched Mike
Tyson with a stiff left uppercut and floored the champ. The blow K-O'd
Tyson and earned 29-year-old Douglas the heavyweight belt. Before the
match, many analysts questioned whether Douglas deserved to be in the
same ring as the previously undefeated Tyson. <
    -11-<

Authorities in the kingdom of Nepal are warning university students to NOT join in the nationwide protests that the fledgling political opposition has scheduled for next Sunday. In a sharply worded statement, the government urged students to— quote— ``guard themselves against instigators or undesirable elements.'' Nepalese authorities have detained an estimated 500 pro-reform leaders in the past week. (
     —11—(

New York City Transit cop Thomas Breyer says he sees— quote— ``everything from life to death'' in his line of work. Yesterday, he and his partner, Jerry Lofredo, had a hand in the ``life'' aspect of the job. Responding to a nine-one-one call, the two arrived at a Manhattan subway platform in time to assist an 18-year-old woman give birth. The heads-up officers both had participated in the birth of their own kids. (
     —11—(

Upon his release from prison today (at 8 a-m e-s-t), South African black nationalist Nelson Mandela (Mahn-DEH'-lah) is scheduled to be driven into Cape Town for a news conference and a rally to celebrate his new freedom. Mandela, the symbolic head of the anti-apartheid (Ah-PAHR'-tayt) movement... has been in prison for more than 27 years because of his fight for black self-determination. (
     —11—(

Secretary of State Baker touched down in Bucharest today in the final leg of a weeklong visit to Eastern Europe. Prior to travelling to Romania, aides to Baker say he expressed U-S reservations to Bulgaria's transitional communist government about the way the interim government is preparing for national elections. Baker stressed the importance of free elections to preserve the Bulgarian revolution. (
     —11—(

Seven hours after challenger James ``Buster'' Douglas knocked out champ Mike Tyson, the World Boxing Council and the World Boxing Association declared the world heavyweight championship vacant pending a review of the fight next week. W-B-C and W-B-A officials say they'll review Tyson's claim that the referee gave Douglas more than 10 seconds when he was knocked down in the eighth round. Tyson went down in the 10th. (
     —11—(

The Khmer Rouge (Kuh-MAIR') guerrilla group has tossed a wrench into the Cambodian peace process by announcing its refusal today to take part in peace talks set to begin this month in Indonesia. Khmer radio broadcast excerpts of a letter sent by a rebel leader to the Indonesian foreign minister that rejected the meeting's agenda, rules and participants. Indonesia has held two previous rounds of peace talks. (
     —11—(

Indonesian officials say at least 15 people died and another four-dozen were injured when Mount Kelud (Keh-LOOD') erupted yesterday. Police say the 56-hundred-79-foot in East Java is quiet this morning. Regarded as one of the world's most dangerous volcanos... Kelud spewed lava on nearby towns and rained ash on cities as far as 30 miles away. (
     —11—(

A published report (in The Miami Herald) indicates Miami's bank system leads the nation with a five-point-one-BILLION-dollar surplus, a tell-tale sign of the drug trade. The article states a federal grand jury is looking into at least six area banks in one of the most intensive money-laundering cases in U-S history. A federal official says stemming the flow of money to illegal drug organizations will deliver their death knell. (
     —11—(

The Soviet news agency Tass reports two cosmonauts blasted off today on the sixth manned-mission to the Mir (Meer) space station. The crew will dock the spaceship with the giant orbiting complex Tuesday and replace the two-man crew of the fifth main expedition. This morning's launch comes amid growing criticism by Soviet legislators of the cost of the U-S-S-R space program. (

-11-<
After a three-month introductory period, the nation's third-largest
city took the plunge yesterday and introduced a new area code. While
Chicago will retain its 3-1-2 code, its collar suburbs have changed to a
new one, 7-0-8. The conversion will affect one-point-seven Million
customers and was implemented because Illinois Bell was running out of
phone numbers in the Chicago metropolitan area. <
-11-<
Secretary of State Baker wrapped up his six-day Eastern European
tour by speaking with Romanian leaders for four hours. The interim
government had hoped to use Baker's visit to allay U-S fears regarding
Bucharest's commitment to democratic reforms. Romania is also anxious to
regain most-favored-nation status, which former dictator Nicolae
Ceausescu (NIHK'-oh-ligh Chow-SHEHS'-koo) renounced after U-S criticism
of his human rights record. <
-11-<
West German Chancellor Kohl says Soviet President Gorbachev
(GOHRB'-ah-chawf) has promised to let Germans determine the time frame
for German reunification. Kohl's announcement came after a one-day visit
to Moscow. Gorbachev's acceptance of a unified German state reverses a
45-year-old policy and could carry for him enormous political risk since
more than 20-Million Soviets died in World War Two. <
-11-<
Heavy artillery fell silent today in east Beirut after one week of
fighting between rival Christian forces. But the head of the Lebanese
Forces militia says he doubts if the tense peace will hold due to the
''destructive and suicidal policy'' of his foe, General Michel Aoun
(MEE'-shehl Aw-OON'). Samir Geagea also invited Syrian troops to join
him in his attempt to quell Aoun. <
-11-<
The left uppercut that James ''Buster'' Douglas delivered in the
10th round of the heavyweight title fight in Tokyo accomplished two
firsts- it floored champ Mike Tyson and knocked him out as well. But
Douglas is NOT the new champ. The World Boxing Council and the World
Boxing Association say the throne is vacant pending a review of a
complaint lodged by Tyson that Douglas was given more than 10 seconds to
get up after Tyson decked him in the eighth round. <
-11-<
Texas law enforcement officials capped a two-year federally funded
drug investigation yesterday by seizing 132 pounds of methamphetamine
hidden in a San Antonio storage facility. Undercover agents staged the
raid based on information obtained Friday when they arrested a San
Antonio couple for drug possession. The head of the Alamo Area Narcotics
Task Force says the seized narcotics have an estimated street value of
20-Million dollars. <
-11-<
Coast Guard officials are trying to determine how an anchor
punctured the hull of an oil tanker last Wednesday and caused a gigantic
oil spill that has fouled 13 miles of Southern California's coast.
Nearly 400-thousand gallons of oil spilled through two holes 38-feet
beneath the surface in the side of the U-S-registered tanker American
Trader. Cleanup efforts are underway. <
-11-<
A man named James ''Buster'' Douglas knocked out heavyweight
champion Mike Tyson last night in the 10th round of their title bout in
Tokyo. Until then, Tyson had been undefeated. It was surely one of the
most stunning and controversial upsets in boxing history. But just hours
after Douglas flattened Tyson, the World Boxing Council and the World
Boxing Association declared their championships vacant... pending a
review of an eighth-round Tyson knockdown of Douglas. Tyson says in his
heart he feels like he's still the champion. <
-11-<

Secretary of State Baker wrapped up a six-day tour of Eastern Europe today that included clashes with senior Soviet officials in Moscow over U-S defense policy. Baker held four hours of talks with Romanian leaders before leaving Bucharest for Shannon, Ireland, where he's expected to stop briefly before returning home. Baker is the highest-ranking U-S official to visit Romania since the December revolution that toppled communist dictator Nicolae Ceausescu (NIHK'-oh-ligh Chow-SHEHS'-koo). <
  -11- <

An East Berlin newspaper quotes a leading adviser to Soviet President Gorbachev (GOHRB'-ah-chawf) as saying the Soviet Union won't stand in the way of German reunification so long as the interests of Germany's neighbors are taken into account. The paper quotes Valentin Falin as saying Moscow does NOT favor the removal of troops from East Germany if American troops remain on West German soil. Western experts estimate there are 350-thousand Soviet troops stationed in East Germany. The United States has over 240-thousand troops stationed in West Germany. <
  -11- <

The East German news agency (A-D-N) reports more than 100 East Germans protested outside the Soviet Embassy in East Berlin, demanding the removal of Soviet helicopters from a city near the border with Poland. Protesters say the Soviets pulled tanks out of Prenzlau, but left military helicopters. The news agency says one Soviet tank divison stationed left the area May 18th as part of Soviet President Gorbachev's (GOHRB'-ah-chawfs) unilateral troop reductions. <
  -11- <

Secretary of State Baker will begin his journey home today after a final stop in Shannon, Ireland. Baker held four hours of talks with Romanian leaders today as he ended a six-day tour of Eastern Europe that included debate with senior Soviet officials over U-S defense policy. <
  -11- <

Reports from Tehran say Iran marked the 11th anniversary of its revolution today with marches and a mass rally in the capital. The rally culminates 11 days of ceremonies in Tehran, where anniversary celebrations were held for the first time since the Ayatollah Khomeini (Ah-yah-toh-LAH' Khoh-may-nee) died in June of last year. <
  -11- <

Two Soviet cosmonauts blasted off today for the Mir (Meer) space station where two other cosmonauts are waiting to come back to earth after six months in orbit. The Soviet news agency Tass says the rocket rumbled off the ground from a launch pad in Soviet Central Asia. <
  -11- <

Tennessee's only black congressman goes on trial tomorrow in Memphis on fraud charges. Representative Harold Ford is accused of taking one-and-a-half Million dollars in fraudulent bank loans to mobilize his political machine behind a candidate for governor. The 44-year-old flamboyant eight-term Democrat says he's innocent and accuses the government's chief prosecutor of waging a personal vendetta against him. <
  -11- <

Federal health officials say this year may be a repeat of the resurgence of measles that hit Americans in 1989. The Centers for Disease Control says there has already been three times more reported cases of measles than last year at this time. Last year's 17-thousand cases included at least 42 deaths. <
  -11- <

Bush administration sources say President Bush and the leaders of
three Andean nations will agree to unprecedented steps in the war on
drugs at a summit in Colombia this week. The sources say the leaders
will sign an already drafted document that would have the United States
backing efforts to replace the South American drug trade with legal
commerce. Thursday's meeting will involve Colombia, Peru and Bolivia—
the world's biggest cocaine producers... and the United States— the
drug's biggest consumer. (
 -11-(
Secretary of State Baker talked with Romanian opposition leaders
today before leaving Bucharest. Some of the opposition leaders asked
Baker for U-S help in such basics as supplying typewriters and typing
paper... as well as instruction in how to go about establishing a new
set of laws. Baker promised Romania 80-Million dollars in humanitarian
food aid before concluding his six-day trip of Eastern Europe. Baker is
now headed to an international conference in Canada. (
 -11-(
State police in Illinois are looking for six prisoners who escaped
from the Joliet Correctional Center near Chicago today. A nationwide
alert has been issued for the prisoners, three of whom are considered
extremely dangerous. Those three, all convicted murderers, are Daniel
Johnson, James Allen and David Rodriguez. The other three are Tommy
Munoz, Ron Roach and Terry Colburn. Police say the six cut through bars
and a fence to escape the facility, which is about 45 miles southwest of
Chicago. (
 -11-(
West German Chancellor Helmut Kohl today ended a two-day visit to
Moscow, saying Soviet President Gorbachev (GOHRB'-ah-chawf) promised him
to leave the time frame for German reunification for Germans to decide.
Kohl told a news conference that West Germany and East Germany would
again be one nation in the near future. The agreement on reunification
reversed the Soviets' 45-year refusal to allow a reunited Germany to
prevent any chance of a powerful Germany again posing a miltary threat
to the Soviet Union. (
 -11-(
In Chicago, authorities say three children died in a smoky
apartment fire possibly started by children playing with matches.
Authorities also say an 18-year-old woman and her infant daughter were
injured in the blaze that swept through a West Side apartment early
today. Fire officials say the fire started in a closet of the first
floor rear apartment. (
 -11-(
South Africa is receiving praise on Capitol Hill today for its
release of black nationalist leader Nelson Mandela. However, lawmakers
appear unwilling to call for the immediate easing of sanctions against
the white minority government. In the words of one lawmaker— ''the fact
is that South Africa is still NOT free.'' (
 -11-(
Bush administration sources say a document being prepared for this
week's hemispheric drug summit in Colombia commits the United States,
Colombia, Peru and Bolivia to share more intelligence information in the
war on drugs. All three countries will require stricter registration of
planes and ships... used to smuggle narcotics. (
 -11-(
The American manufacturers of Perrier water says the source of
small amounts of benzene in bottles of the mineral water has been traced
to the bottling process in France. Though NO benzene has been detected
in European samples, the company plans to stop production world-wide
until the source of the chemical has been isolated. (
 -11-(

Secretary of State Baker promised 80-Million dollars in aid to Romania, which is running out of food and energy. The aid includes 500-thousand tons of grain and 75-hundred tons of butter. Baker says more aid would depend on more reforms. Baker left Bucharest today, ending a tour of Eastern Europe. ‹

  —11—‹

Japan's prime minister told a disappointingly small crowd today that Japan needs to stay with the ruling party that brought the nation out of poverty to the world's second-strongest economic power. Polls show the socialists and other opposition parties with an even chance of winning next week's elections. ‹

  —11—‹

Rebels in Ethiopia are once again claiming to have captured the Red Sea port of Massawa (Mah-SAH'-wah). But the Soviet-backed government denies the claim... which the rebels have made twice before. The government says three days of fighting by rebels threatens vital food-supply lines to food-starved areas. ‹

  —11—‹

Commentator Andy Rooney says he feels like Salman Rushdie (SAHL'-muhn RUHSH'-dee), the British author who remains in hiding after offending Iranian leaders with his book, ``The Satanic Verses.'' Rooney denies in today's syndicated column that he made racist remarks that caused C-B-S to suspend him for three months. ‹

WORLD ROUNDUP

  —11—‹

(Drugsummit) ‹

Bush administration sources say ``a document of agreements'' being prepared for this week's drug summit in Colombia will commit the United States, Colombia, Peru and Bolivia to ``unprecedented'' co-operation in the war on drugs. ‹

The sources say the United States will bolster efforts to halt the smuggling of U-S-made weapons to South American drug lords and limit the export of chemicals used to make cocaine. ‹

The United States will also attempt to shift farmers away from growing cocaine crops with a plan to replace the illegal South American drug trade with legal commerce such as fruits and textiles. ‹

In return... Colombia, Peru and Bolivia will share more intelligence with the United States... the world's biggest cocaine consumer. ‹

All three countries will promise to crack down on the laundering of drug money and will require stricter registration of planes and ships that are often used to smuggle narcotics. ‹

  ‹

Secretary of State Baker brought news of 80-Million dollars in humanitarian food aid to Romania today. But Baker warned the communist leaders that if they want any more U-S aid, they'll have to have free elections and make more progress toward a free-market economy. ‹

Baker also met with 40 opposition leaders. One student leader told Baker that Romanians want the United States to be ``tough'' and refuse to accept the communist interim government. The student leader described the older leaders in the transitional government as ``the old element... communists who have served before and failed.'' ‹

Baker's pledge of aid includes 500-thousand tons of grain and 75-hundred tons of butter. The Romanian capital of Bucharest is already experiencing some food and energy shortages. The food will be either given outright to needy Romanians or will be paid for in Romanian currency... with the proceeds going for economic development projects in Romania. ‹

Some opposition leaders asked Baker for U-S help in such elemental areas as supplying typewriters and typing paper and instruction on how to establish a new code of laws. (
 -11-(
 (Voyager)(—
 NASA scientists will turn on cameras aboard the space agency's aging Voyager-1 probe Tuesday for a final set of pictures before Voyager-1 drifts out into space. (
 The last time Voyager-1 was in the news was 10 years ago when it was taking pictures of Saturn and Saturn's moon Titan. (
 The Voyager-1 was launched in 1977 and since its encounter with Saturn... it's been drifting out to a position in space above the plane of our solar system. It's all set to take a so-called ``family portrait'' of the sun and... scientists hope... seven of the nine planets. (
 Only Jupiter will show a clearly discernible disk. Earth will show up only as a brilliant star-like point of light. (
 Voyager-1 will take 64 pictures of the solar system over a four-hour period. The images will be stored on tape until the end of March... when they will be radioed back to Earth. The first pictures will be released to the public in late April. (
 -11-(
 (Nato)(
 The issue of German re-unification was on the agenda this weekend as President Bush and NATO Secretary General Manfred Woerner (MAHN'-frehd VEHR'-nehr) conferred at Camp David, Maryland. (
 Both men restated the cautious Western approach to what has become known as ``the German question'' in language that underscored the uncertain course of political change. (
 They thanked the West German government for assuring that a unified Germany would remain a member of NATO. (
 At the same time... they agreed that NATO... in addition to maintaining the common defense... should adopt new political roles to meet a changing Europe. And they say NATO should play a strong role in discussion on arms cuts. (
 Soviet Foreign Ministry spokesman Gennady Gerasimov (Gehn-NAH'-dee Gehr-AH'-see-mawf) says (on A-B-C) many Soviets are un-easy with the notion of a reunified Germany because the Soviet Union lost 20-Million people in World War Two. (
 -11-(
 (Valentines)(
 British monarchs apparently are as susceptible as their commoners to the pleasures of love, as well as its silliness. (
 That's what's apparent from their love letters, as seen in a collection at London's Royal Britain exhibition. It spans more than 450 years, and is in honor of Valentine's Day. (
 One letter was written in 1528 from King Henry the Eighth to Anne Boleyn, who was then his mistress. Says Henry- ``Wishing myself- specially in evening- in my sweetheart's arms.'' He signed it- ``Written with the hand of him that was, is and shall be yours by his will. H-R''(
 She became Henry's second wife, but he later had her beheaded because she had NOT borne him a son. (
 Another letter is from Prince Albert to Queen Victoria, shortly before their marriage. Said Albert- ``Dearest, best beloved Victoria. Already another dear, dear letter from you which has wholly charmed me, for it once again tells me you love me.''(
 Other letters are from King Edward the Eighth, who abdicated in 1936 for American divorcee Wallis Simpson. In one written in 1937, he lapses into silliness, saying- ``My Sweetheart. This is just to say good meesel and that I love you more and more before I take another drowsel.''(

SPORTS

-11-‹

(Box-Heavy)‹

James ``Buster'' Douglas rocked the boxing world Sunday in Japan. Douglas took the heavyweight championship from previously UNbeaten Mike Tyson with a stunning 10th-round knockout in the Tokyo Dome. Douglas entered the fight a prohibitive underdog, but took command at the opening bell and thoroughly befuddled the 23-year-old champion. ‹

Although he was dominant, the 29-year-old challenger from Columbus, Ohio, did go down in the eighth round and Tyson came out looking for the kill in the ninth. But the inspired Douglas used a 12-inch reach advantage to land five straight punches that backed up Tyson and completey closed the left eye. In the final round, Douglas knew he had Tyson in trouble and landed a left, then a combination that ended with a decisive uppercut. And the fight was over. ‹

‹

Tyson became the youngest heavyweight champion when he stopped Trevor Berbick in two rounds November 22nd, 1986, to claim the World Boxing Council title as a 20-year-old. He later went on to win both the World Boxing Association and International Boxing Federation crowns. The Douglas fight was Tyson's 10th title defense and came on the heels of six straight knockouts. He registered 33 knockouts in his 37 victories before Douglas turned the tables. Douglas, himself, now is 30-4-1. ‹

‹

The only betting on the fight, expected to be a tuneup for a June 18th title defense against top-ranked challenger Evander Holyfield, was on whether the bout would last four rounds. ‹

-11-‹

(NHL)‹

In the N-H-L last night, Pittsburgh's Mario Lemieux (Luhe-MYOO') extended his scoring streak to 45 games to move within six games of tying the all-time record. Lemieux assisted on Paul Coffey's second-period goal to help the Pens chalk up a 7-6 victory over the Los Angeles Kings, whose captain Wayne Gretzky holds the record Lemiuex is trying to break. NOT to be forgotten is Pittsburgh's Rob Brown, who sealed the victory by completing a hat trick. ‹

‹

Elsewhere on the ice, Hartford mauled Toronto 6-2... Montreal embarrassed Quebec 7-2... and St. Louis tamed New Jersey 7-0. In afternoon play, Detroit out-lasted Calgary 7-5... the New York Islanders trimmed Boston 4-3 in overtime... and Minnesota out-gunned Chicago 6-4. ‹

'-11-‹

(NBA Stars)‹

The N-B-A's weekend extravaganza in Miami winds up today (at 3 p-m, E-S-T) with the 40th annual All Star Game matching the elite from the Eastern and Western Conferences. The West captured last season's classic 143-134, but the East leads the overall series 25-14. ‹

‹

Detroit's Coach Chuck Daly will coach the East squad and a starting lineup of New York's Patrick Ewing at center, Larry Bird of Boston and Charles Barkley of Philadelphia at forward... and Michael Jordan of Chicago and Isiah Thomas of the Pistons at guard. ‹

Pat Riley of the Los Angeles Lakers is coaching the West for the sixth straight time and this year has three of his own players in the starting lineup. The Lakers getting the nod in the fan vote are guard Magic Johnson and forwards James Worthy and A-C Green. Houston center Akeem Olajuwon (Oh-LIGH'-kah-wahn) and guard John Stockton of Utah round out the starting five. ‹

-11-‹

(NBA Weekend)<
Miami's All Star Weekend began yesterday with a series of fun
events, including the crowd-pleasing Slam Dunk Contest won for the
second time by Dominique Wilkins of the Atlanta Hawks. Craig Hodges of
the Chicago Bulls won the three-point shooting contest, with former
champion Larry Bird of Boston and newcomer Michael Jordan of Bulls far
out of the running. Earlier, Cazzie Russell's basket with 17 seconds
remaining gave the East a 37-36 victory over the West in the Legends
Old-Timers Game. <
   -11-<
(College BKB)<
Arkansas' hoped-for march up the ladder to an eventual number-one
billing was rudely halted yesterday by the youthful Baylor Bears.
Baylor, struggling to break even in the Southwest Conference, shocked
the third-ranked Hogs 82-77. The Bears were fueled by sophomore guard
David Wesley, who scored 23 points, including four on clutch free throws
in the last minute. The decision ends the nation's longest current
winning streak at 12 games and drops the Razorbacks to 20-3 overall and
11-1 in the S-W-C. <
   <
   The pollsters also were looking at a pair of Big Eight games
involving top-ranked Missouri and number two Kansas. Missouri ripped
Nebraska 107-85 and Kansas got by Iowa State 88-83. But Missouri's
stunning loss to Kansas State earlier this week now apparently clears
the way for the Jayhawks to regain the number-one slot they held for
much of the early season. <
   <
   Looking at the other members of the U-P-I poll in action, it was
number four Duke nudging Maryland 114-111 in overtime... number five
Georgetown dropping Florida 56-40 in a real slow-down affair... number
six Syracuse tripping number 11 Connecticut 90-86 in a Big East
battle... and number seven Nevada-Las Vegas routing Oklahoma State
100-84. <
   In the second half of the ratings, it was number 12 L-S-U
out-gunning Tennessee 119-113... number 15 Georgia Tech nailing
14th-ranked Louisville 94-84... number 16 La Salle blasting Manhatttan
99-78... number 19 New Mexico State inching by Cal-Santa Barbara
66-64... and number 20 U-C-L-A falling to Arizona 83-74. <
   -11-<
(PGA)<
Hubert Green holds a one-stroke lead over David Ishii (EE'-shee)
entering today's final round of Hawaiian Open Golf Championship in
Honolulu. Green finished with a six-under-par 66 yesterday... thanks to
an eagle on the 18th hole. The former champion stands at 10-under 206
overall for the edge on Ishii, who turned in a 68. Paul Azinger
(AY'-zihn-gehr) and second-round leader Craig Stadler are next on the
list at 210. <
   -11-<
(PGASenior)<
Mike Hill is two shots ahead of the field approaching today's
closing round of the Suncoast Seniors Golf Classic. Hill moved to the
front with yesterday's three-under-par 69. Dale Douglass and Larry Mowry
are tied for second with five-under-par totals of 139. Lee Trevino and
Gary Player both are within striking distance, three strokes off the
lead. <
   -11-<
(Tennis)<
Tim Mayotte faces top seed Ivan Lendl today in the final of the
Stella Artois (Ahr-TWAH') Italian Indoor tennis tournament in Milan.
Mayotte advanced to the finals by surprising John McEnroe in the
semifinals yesterday by twin scores of 6-4. Lendl chopped off U-S
teen-ager Pete Sampras after a slow start by a score of 3-6, 6-love,
6-3. <

<

Lendl announced yesterday he'll return to his native Czechoslovakia
later this month for the first time since 1984 to play an exhibition
match against Miroslav Mecir (MEER'-oh-slahv MAY'-cheer) in Prague.
Lendl has lived in Connecticut for years and will receive U-S
citizenship in 1992. He says he accepted the invitation as a consequence
of the recently adopted political reforms. <
    -11-<
(US Figures—Men) <
The U-S Figure Skating Championships wind up today in Salt Lake
City with the men's final. But defending champion Chris Bowman is
UNcertain if he will able to take the ice for the scheduled free skating
program. Bowman is suffering from a recurring back problem and fell out
of contention after a nightmarish original program Friday night...
virtually handing the 1990 title to either young Todd Eldredge or
veteran Paul Wylie. <
    -11-<
(US Figures—Women) <
Jill Trenary (TREHN'-ahr-ee) scoffed at the so-called experts who
questioned her toughness and yesterday won her third U-S Figure Skating
Championship. Trenary went into the finals in Salt Lake City leading
teenagers Tyna Harding by just two-tenths of a factored place and Kristi
Yamaguchi (Yah-mah-GOO'-chee) by four-10ths. The 21-year-old Colorado
Springs star responded by combining five clean triple jumps with her
elegant artistry to claim the title. Yamaguchi settled for the silver
medal... while Harding faltered and came in seventh overall... leaving
Holly Cooke with the brozne. <
    -11-<
(Skiing) <
Carole Merle of France completed her comeback from last year's
severe knee injury by capturing the women's World Cup Super Giant Slalom
yesterday. She shaved·Switzerland's Maria Walliser (VAHL'-ihs-ehr) by
two-one-hundredths of a second on the Meribel, France, course which will
be used in the 1992 Olympics. <
    -11-<
(Daytona) <
Ken Schrader (SHRAY'-dehr) loves to race at Daytona— as long as
he's the only one on the track. Schrader won his third straight pole for
the Daytona 500 yesterday with a speed of more than 196 miles an hour
and will lead the field next Sunday. But Schrader has NEVER won a
Winston Cup race at Daytona. <
<
At the Daytona track today, Jimmy Hensley leads the field in the
20-lap Busch Clash. Schrader starts third. And Patty Moise starts in
front in today's 80-lap ARCA race. A six-car accident in practice run
caused three drivers to scratch yesterday— including Ritchie Petty. <
    -11-<
(PBA) <
Freehold, New Jersey, bowler Parker Bohn the Third won the P-B-A
Don Carter Classic in Kenner, Louisiana. The veteran bowler out of
Freehold, New Jersey, defeated Mike Edwards 214-191 in the title match.
Jeff Bellinger beat Steve Wunderlich and Amleto Monacelli (Am-LEH'-toh
Mohn-ah-SHEHL'-oh) in the semifinals before losing to Edwards. <
    -11-<
(Pirates) <
The Pittsburgh Pirates won one and lost one in a pair of
arbitration rulings. Part-time outfielder R-J Reynolds lost his bid for
a big raise and will have to settle for 535-thousand dollars this year.
But pitcher Bob Kipper won his case and will earn 525-thousand. The Bucs
had offered a salary of 380-thousand. <
    -11-<

(Vikings)〈
All-Pro defensive end Chris Doleman of the Vikings is heading to
court in his bid to be declared a free agent. A Minnesota judge will
decide tomorrow whether the Vikings are entitled to hold Doleman to an
option year on his three-year contract. Doleman says he did NOT agree to
the option year. The Vikings maintain he signed a contract including an
option clause. 〈
　-11-〈
　(Birthday)〈
Our birthday greetings today (Sunday)... February 11th... go out to
N-B-A Hall of Famer Bill Russell. He is 56 years old. 〈
　-11-〈
**Here is SportsTalk, the lighter side... the sports people...
controversy... the oddities... by United Press International.** 〈
〈
NOT long ago, track and field athletes were competing for money
under the table. Now, they are openly running for dollars. 〈
The 250-thousand dollars in bonus money available Friday at the
Vitalis Meadowlands Invitational is evidence of the direction of track
and field. 〈
Last month, the Sunkist Invitational offered one-Million dollars
for a world record in the men's mile. Last summer, the Jack-in-the-Box
meet in Los Angeles offered 500-thousand for anyone who could break Bob
Beamon's long jump world record. 〈
The sport needs these incentives to attract top athletes and
produce superior marks. It also creates interest and excitement among
the crowds, who cheer harder when they know so much money is on the
line. 〈
The 12-thousand at the Meadowlands urged on Romanian Doina Melinte
during her world-record mile run... and did the same for England's Peter
Elliott in his bid to break the world mark in the men's mile. 〈
Melinte earned 100-thousand for breaking her own world record in
the mile. She clocked four minutes 17-point-13 seconds to erase the mark
of four-18-86 she set at the Meadowlands two years ago. 〈
Elliott came within about two seconds of another bonanza. His
winning time of three-52-oh-two fell short of the time he needed to
break Eamonn Coghlan's world record of three-49-78 and claim the
100-thousand-dollar bonus. 〈
　-11-〈
A Chesapeake, Virginia, couple say stray golf balls create an
airborne assault on their home. They want the eighth hole shut down at
Seven Springs Golf Club. 〈
Arthur and Marilyn O'Connell have filed a lawsuit and maintain that
since 1987 they have been bombarded frequently by golf balls missing the
green a few yards from their property. They contend the balls and the
golfers are trespassers and the wayward shots create an unsafe nuisance.
But, the owner of the golf course says balls in their yard are par
for the course. He says when they built the house, they knew it was on a
golf course. You can't live on a golf course and complain about golf
balls. It's like living on the ocean and complaining about the sand. 〈
　-11-〈
　(Fan Fact)〈
A current star holds the record for most assists in an N-B-A
All-Star Game. 〈
Can you name the player?〈
〈
Magic Johnson of the Los Angeles Lakers had 22 assists in the 1984
game won by the East 154-145 in overtime. 〈
　-11-〈
A leaf from the memory book of sports...〈
〈
Pat Riley blends city slicker looks with country boy values... and
is contemplating life without Magic. And he's smiling. 〈

It's the smile of an N-B-A coach who boasts the highest lifetime winning percentage in both regular season and playoff history without much Forum fanfare. 〈

The Lakers have won four N-B-A titles under Riley's direction, earning Team of the Decade honors for the 1980's. On Sunday, Riley will coach the Western Conference All-Stars for the sixth straight season and eighth overall... with three Lakers in his starting lineup. 〈

30-year-old Magic Johnson is in his 11th pro season and became the team's unquestioned focal point when Kareem Abdul-Jabbar slowed noticeably three years ago. Johnson won a championship ring under Paul Westhead as a rookie in 1980, then added four more with Riley as head coach. 〈

Riley has never won N-B-A Coach of the Year honors, and may never enjoy the opportunity to sneak up on someone. His Lakers are always expected to win the league championship. And they usually do. 〈

Riley says- ``This franchise has been way up there for 11 years now and we've got another three or four years at the top before we might have to deal with Magic being gone.'' 〈

-11-〈

The W-B-C and W-B-A world heavyweight titles are in limbo. The organizations declared their championships vacant pending a review of today's eighth-round Mike Tyson knockdown by James ``Buster'' Douglas in Tokyo. 〈
〈

Douglas apparently became the new heavyweight champ of the world when he knocked out Tyson in the 10th round. But, the referee admitted starting the 10-count late in the eighth round, giving Douglas extra time to get up. 〈
-0-〈

The N-B-A All-Star Game is today in Miami. Yesterday, Atlanta's Dominique Wilkins won the slam dunk contest, Chicago's Craig Hodges won the three-point shooting contest, and the East beat the West in the old-timers game. 〈
-0-〈

In college basketball today, 13th-ranked Illinois visits eighth-rated Michigan, number nine Purdue is at 18th-ranked Minnesota, 10th-rated Oklahoma calls on Seton Hall and 17th-ranked Oregon State hosts Oregon. 〈
-0-〈

Buffalo Sabres winger Alexander Mogilny (Moh-GIHL'-nee), apparently afraid of flying, did NOT accompany the team to St. Louis for tonight's game against the Blues. There's also a report that Mogilny plans to quit the N-H-L club. 〈
-11-〈

(Daytona) 〈

Ken Schrader beat fellow Chevrolet driver Greg Sacks by two car lengths today to win his second straight Busch Clash stock car race at Daytona International Speedway. 〈

Schrader passed Sacks for the lead on the fifth lap and domininated the remainder of the 20-lap, 50-mile race for 1989 pole winners. He averaged more than 192 miles per hour and collected a record 95-thousand dollars. 〈

Davey Allison finished third ahead of fellow Ford drivers Geoff Bodine (Boh-DIGHN'), Bill Elliott, Mark Martin and Alan Kulwicki. 〈

Schrader claimed his third straight Daytona 500 pole yesterday. He earned a 10-thousand-dollar bonus for leading the fifth lap of today's race, a 15-thousand-dollar bonus for leading lap 10 and another 10-thousand for leading the 15th lap. 〈
-11-〈

(Sabres-Sub) <
    A Buffalo newspaper (News) reports that forward Alexander Mogilny
(Moh-GIHL'-nee) of the Buffalo Sabres may quit the N-H-L team. <
    Mogilny apparently suffers from a serious fear of flying and did
NOT accompany the Sabres to St. Louis for tonight's game against the
Blues. <
    According to the newspaper, Mogilny was overheard by teammates as
saying during Friday night's home game against the New York Rangers that
the game would be his last as a Sabre. <
    Mogilny defected from the Soviet Union last year and missed one
road trip with the Sabres earlier this season, reportedly because of a
stomach virus that had been aggravated by his fear of flying. <
    Mogilny has 10 goals and 19 assists in 47 games this season.
Buffalo General Manager Gerry Meehan said late last night that he did
NOT expect Mogilny to quit the team. <
    -11-<
    (Menten) <
    Ivan Lendl, the world's top-ranked men's tennis player, picked up
his second tournament title of the year today with a 6-3, 6-2 win over
American Tim Mayotte in the final of the Italian Indoor Championship at
Milan. <
    Lendl earned 78-thousand dollars for his 85th career title. He has
now beaten Mayotte in 16 straight matches. <
    Lendl won the Australian Open earlier this year and his main goal
is to win Wimbledon for the first time. <
    Mayotte advanced to the title match with A 6-4, 6-4 Victory over
John McEnroe in yesterday's semifinals, while Lendl outlasted American
teenager Pete Sampras, 3-6, 6-love, 6-3. <

r s Sports-Figures 0100
    (SALT LAKE CITY)- A bad back has forced defending champion Chris
Bowman to withdraw from today's final round of the U-S men's figure
skating championships at Salt Lake City. Bowman is in fourth place in
the overall standings and out of reach of the gold medal. He fell and
turned in a dismal performance on Friday night in the original, or
short, program portion of the men's three-round competition. Bowman's
tough luck paved the way to a gold medal win by either 18-year-old Todd
Eldredge or veteran Paul Wylie. <

CONSUMER

    -12-<
    The Food and Drug Administration says health claims by food
companies are getting out of hand. <
    The F-D-A is proposing regulations that would limit such claims to
well-documented links between food and health such as fat and heart
disease. The rules would replace a 1987 plan enacted under the Reagan
administration that allows health claims for food products. The move led
to an avalanche of labels and advertisements touting everything from
cereals to margarine as ways to prevent various ailments. <
    The industry estimates that nearly 40 percent of new food products
introduced in the first half of 1989 carried health claims. And it's
estimated that one-third of the three-point-six-BILLION dollars spent on
food advertising now features health-related messages. <
    Before the Reagan administration, the F-D-A did NOT allow companies
to make claims linking food to the prevention or treatment of a
particular disease. <

Says Health and Human Services Secretary Sullivan- ``In hindsight, the 1987 proposal has proved to be too permissive.'' <

Sullivan says he wants the government to make a mid-course correction to determine what health messages will and will NOT be allowed. <

The new F-D-A plan would allow companies to make health claims only if they fall within a range of relationships between diet and health. <

The F-D-A plans to consider claims concerning six areas. They are- fat and heart disease... fiber and heart disease... salt and high blood pressure... fats and cancer... fiber and cancer... and calcium and osteoporosis. <

The new proposal will be published in the Federal Register this week, and there will be a 60-day comment period after that. <

-12- <

End-Today's-Consumer <

<

FINANCIAL

-12- <

There was a small gain on Wall Street last Friday after earlier profit-taking was reported. The Dow Industrials were up three-point-83 to 26-hundred-48-point-20 in moderate trade of 146-point-nine-Million shares. Advances led declines by 102 issues. <

-O- <

Automobile insurance rates have been frozen in Georgia on orders from Insurance Commissioner Warren Evans. He has been under fire recently because of the high rates paid in the state. <

<

Average car insurance rates in Georgia increased by five-point-45 percent in 1988. Costs jumped nearly 109 percent from 1982 to 1988. <

-O- <

Home ownership became slightly more expensive last week, according to the Federal Home Loan Mortgage Corporation. ``Freddie Mac,'' as it's known, buys mortgages from lenders... packaging them as securities for sale to investors. <

<

Fixed rate mortgages increased by four-hundredths of one percentage to 10-point-21 percent. Adjustable-rate mortgage rates were up one-one-hundredth of one percentage point to eight-point-46 percent. <

(LONDON)- The dollar opened mostly lower today against major European currencies. Gold prices were mixed. <

In Tokyo, the Tokyo Foreign Exchange closed today because of a national holiday. Trading will resume tomorrow. <

Gold opened unchanged in Zurich at 416 dollars an ounce. London gold opened down) at 415 dollars 25 cents an ounce against 415 dollars 75 cents. <

Silver opened lower in Zurich at five dollars 25 cents an ounce against five dollars 30 cents, but was unchanged in London to five dollars 27 cents. <

The London gold price was fixed at 415 dollars 25 cents. down 50 cents. <

London mid-morning spot silver was five dollars 27 cents. <

WEATHER

The National Weather Service reports that yesterday's highest temperature reading in the 48 adjacent United States was 88 degrees fahrenheit (31 Celsius) in Melbourne, Florida. Today's low was seven degrees below zero (MINUS 22 C.) in International Falls, Minnesota. ‹

A cold front dumped snow and rain across the Pacific Northwest today, lifting rivers up to five feet above flood stage, while a heat wave blazed through Texas and temperatures dipped below zero in the Great Lakes. ‹

In the Washington Cascades mountain range, plummeting freezing levels solidified packed snow and relieved the danger of avalanches at Snoqualmie Pass and White Pass, which had been closed over the weekend. ‹

The National Weather Service issued flood warnings for Washington's Snoqualmie, Skookumchuck, Chehalis and White Rivers. The most severe flooding occurred at Centralia when the Chehalis crested five feet above its 65-foot flood stage. ‹

Clear skies prevailed in the nation's midsection but temperatures dropped intosingle digits in northern Wisconsin and down to 1 below in Marquette, Michigan. The mercury rose into the upper 20's to lower 30's in Illinois and Indiana, and were in the 40's in Missouri. ‹

A February heat wave continued in Texas, as a high pressure ridge lingeredover most of the state. Temperatures in the 70's and 80's were common Sunday, with readings of 85 degrees recorded in Alice, Kingsville, Laredo and McAllen. ‹

Springlike sunshine also produced temperatures well above seasonal normals in Oklahoma. Highs ranged from 76 degrees at McAlester to 68 in Guymon Sunday. ‹

In Southern California, it was sunny and warm with temperatures in the 70's and low 80's as the weekend came to an end but a long stretch of summery weather was expected to come to an abrupt end today as a storm moved down from the Pacific Northwest. ‹

Skies are clear over most of the South with temperatures on the chilly side, reaching 43 in Knoxville, Tennessee, 45 in Atlanta, 47 in Charleston, South Carolina, 49 in Jacksonville, Florida, and 63 in Miami. ‹

Seasonably cool temperatures and clear skies prevailed throughout the Northeast and middle Atlantic states, with temperatures ranging from a high of 38 degrees in Washington, D-C, and Roanoke, Virginia, to a low of 23 degrees in Hartford, Connecticut. ‹

Light snow drifted into the New York City area while rain fell in Atlantic City, New Jersey. Clear skies were reported in Philadelphia, where the temperature hovered around 37 degrees. ‹

TODAY'S PEOPLE

-12-‹

The known and the unknown... people making news, next, from United Press International. ‹

‹

This Thursday is Dorothy Mackey Day in the town of Wooster, Ohio, which is honoring the 79-year-old woman for her tireless work helping the homeless. She began back in 1941 when she opened her home to a man who'd been injured in an industrial accident and had NO place to go. Since then, she's offered food and shelter to an estimated 10-thousand people in Wooster, which has NO public-financed shelter for the

homeless. Community action director Brenda Conrad says she doesn't know what Wooster would do without Mackey, who she says ''has borne the load for a long time.'' Mackey herself says she's starting to think about getting some help. She says maybe it's time others started thinking about taking over her job. ‹
‹
A very pregnant woman who was waiting for a New York subway train ended up missing the train— she had a baby instead. The 18-year-old woman delivered her baby on a Seventh Avenue subway platform in Manhattan on Saturday... with the help of transit police. The two officers who assisted said they were well-versed in emergency medical techniques. Neither had delivered a baby while on duty, but both had taken part in the births of their own children. Said one— ''Tonight, we feel real good.'' ‹
‹
There's a possibility BILLIONAIRE developer Donald Trump and his wife WON'T be exchanging Valentines this year. A report out of New York (in the Daily News) says Trump's wife, Ivana, is dumping him because she found out he was cheating on her. The report says Ivana has been so busy raising the couple's three children and serving as her husband's business partner that she only recently realized her 12-year marriage was in trouble. Ivana refused to comment on the report, and Trump is in Tokyo and could NOT be reached for comment. In the past, he's been linked romantically with actress Catherine Oxenberg and ice skater Peggy Fleming. ‹

Ex-wives of the rich and famous will get a chance to speak out tomorrow (Tuesday) when talk-show host Geraldo Rivera does a show featuring them. Guests scheduled to appear include Carol Lawrence, the ex-wife of Robert Goulet... and the ex-wives of Dustin Hoffman, hair ✦ stylist Vidal Sassoon and football stars Mark Gastineau and Joe Montana. Lawrence gives a chilling picture of her marriage to Goulet. She says he would lock their young sons in the trunk of their car and then forget they were there. ‹
(end media attentioner) ‹
‹
Danny Aiello did a lot of things before he became an actor, and some were a bit unsavory. Aiello, who played Sal the pizzeria owner in Spike Lee's ''Do the Right Thing,'' once worked as a bouncer in tough after-hours bars in New York City. In an interview (in People magazine), Aiello says he's ''been shot at,'' and nearly had his ''ear cut off in a fight.'' He said he's even ''broken into other people's houses.'' He was 35 when he decided to try acting. Aiello says he needed a job where he ''could make a lot of money in a short amount of time.'' ‹

Suggested
Readings

Crannell, Kenneth C. *Voice and Articulation*. Belmont, California: Wadsworth Publishing Company, 1987.

Fisher, Hilda B. *Improving Voice and Articulation*. Boston: Houghton Mifflin Company, 1966.

Lessac, Arthur. *The Use and Training of the Human Voice*. New York: DBS Publications, Inc./Drama Book Specialists, 1960.

Linklater, Kristin. *Freeing the Natural Voice*. New York: Drama Book Publishers, 1976.

The Silvananda Companion to Yoga. New York: Simon and Schuster, 1983.

Also Available:

Dr. Utterback has produced a 45-minute audio cassette which serves as a companion guide to *Broadcast Voice Handbook*. This cassette contains dozens of exercises for improving your broadcast voice. To order, send $19.95 plus $2.00 shipping and handling to:

> Bonus Books
> 160 E. Illinois St.
> Chicago, IL 60611

Or save time and call toll-free 1–800–225–3775.

Index